LEADER'S GUIDE

Dr. M. Robert Mulholland, Jr., is a native of Vermont and a graduate of the U.S. Naval Academy, Wesley Theological Seminary, and Harvard University. He is presently vice-president and provost of Asbury Theological Seminary and a professor of New Testament studies. An elder in the Baltimore-Washington Conference of The United Methodist Church, Dr. Mulholland has served in pastoral ministry for nine years and has served on various commissions and task forces of the boards and agencies of The United Methodist Church. He has written two books on spiritual formation: *Shaped by the Word* (Upper Room) and *Invitation to a Journey* (IVP) and is the author of *Revelation: Holy Living in an Unholy World* (Zondervon, 1990).

REVELATION

Copyright © 1996 by Cokesbury
All rights reserved.

JOURNEY THROUGH THE BIBLE: REVELATION. LEADER'S GUIDE. An official resource for The United Methodist Church prepared by the General Board of Discipleship through Church School Publications and published by Cokesbury, The United Methodist Publishing House; 201 Eighth Avenue, South; P.O. Box 801; Nashville, TN 37202-0801. Printed in the United States of America. Copyright ©1996 by Cokesbury.

Scripture quotations in this publication, unless otherwise indicated, are from the New Revised Standard Version of the Bible, copyright ©1989 by the Division of Christian Education of the National Council of the Churches of Christ in the United States of America, and are used by permission. All rights reserved.

For permission to reproduce any material in this publication, call 615-749-6421, or write to Permissions Office, 201 Eighth Avenue, South, P.O. Box 801, Nashville, TN 37202-0801.

To order copies of this publication, call toll free 800-672-1789. Call Monday through Friday 7:00–6:30 Central Time; 5:00–4:30 Pacific Time; Saturday 9:00–5:00. Use your Cokesbury account, American Express, Visa, Discover, or MasterCard.

For information on acquiring this resource in braille, call collect: Trinity Braille Ministry, 602-973-1415.

EDITORIAL AND DESIGN TEAM

Mary Leslie Dawson-Ramsey,
Editor

Linda H. Leach,
Assistant Editor

Linda O. Spicer,
Adult Section Assistant

Ed Wynne,
Layout Designer

Susan J. Scruggs,
Cover Design

ADMINISTRATIVE TEAM

Neil M. Alexander,
Publisher

Duane A. Ewers,
Editor of Church School Publications

Gary L. Ball-Kilbourne,
Senior Editor of Adult Publications

07 08 09 10 – 12 11 10 9 8

CONTENTS

Volume 16: Revelation — by M. Robert Mulholland, Jr.

INTRODUCTION TO THE SERIES

The leader's guides provided for use with JOURNEY THROUGH THE BIBLE make the following assumptions:
- adults learn in different ways:
  —by reading
  —by listening to speakers
  —by working on projects
  —by drama and roleplay
  —by using their imaginations
  —by expressing themselves creatively
  —by teaching others
- the mix of persons in your group is different from that found in any other group.
- the length of the actual time you have for teaching in a session may vary from thirty minutes to ninety minutes.
- the physical place where your class meets is not exactly like the place where any other group or class meets.
- your teaching skills, experiences, and preferences are unlike anyone else's.

We encourage you to discover and develop the ways you can best use the information and learning ideas in this leader's guide with your particular class. To get started, we suggest you try following these steps:

1. Think and pray about your individual class members. Who are they? What are they like? Why are they involved in this particular Bible study class at this particular time in their lives? What seem to be their needs? How do you think they learn best?

2. Think and pray about your class members as a group. A group takes on a character that can be different from the particular characters of the individuals who make up that group. How do your class members interact? What do they enjoy doing together? What would help them become stronger as a group?

3. Keep in mind that you are teaching this class for the sake of the class members, in order to help them increase in their faithfulness as disciples of Jesus Christ. Teachers sometimes fall prey to the danger of teaching in ways that are easiest for themselves. The best teachers accept the discomfort of taking risks and stretching their teaching skills in order to focus on what will really help the class members learn and grow in their faith.

4. Read the chapter in the study book. Read the assigned Bible passages. Read the background Bible passages, if any. Work through the Dimension 1 questions in the study book. Make a list of any items you do not understand and need to research further using such tools as Bible dictionaries, concordances, Bible atlases, and commentaries. In other words, do your homework. Be prepared with your own knowledge about the Bible passages being studied by your class.

5. Read the chapter's material in the leader's guide. You might want to begin with the "Additional Bible Helps," found at the *end* of each chapter. Then look at each learning idea in the "Learning Menu."

6. Spend some time with the "Learning Menu." Notice that the "Learning Menu" is organized around Dimensions 1, 2, and 3 in the study book. Recognizing that different adults and adult classes will learn best using different teaching/learning methods, in each of the three Dimensions you will find
   —at least one learning idea that is primarily discussion-based;
   —at least one learning idea that begins with a method other than discussion, but which may lead into discussion.
   Make notes about which learning ideas will work best given the unique makeup and setting of your class.

7. Decide on a lesson plan. Which learning ideas will you lead the class members through when? What materials will you need? What other preparations do you need to make? How long do you plan to spend on a particular learning idea?

8. Many experienced teachers have found that they do better if they plan more than they actually use during a class session. They also know that their class members may become frustrated if they try to do too much during a class session. In other words
   —plan more than you can actually use. That way, you have back-up learning ideas in case something does not work well or something takes much less time than you thought.
   —don't try to do everything listed in the "Learning Menu." We have intentionally offered you much more than you can use in one class session.
   —be flexible while you teach. A good lesson plan is only a guide for your use as you teach people. Keep the focus on your class members, not your lesson plan.

9. After you teach, evaluate the class session. What worked well? What did not? What did you learn from your experience of teaching that will help you plan for the next class session?

May God's Spirit be upon you as you lead your class on their *Journey Through the Bible*!

Questions or comments? Call Curric-U-Phone 1-800-251-8591.

1

Revelation 1:1-20; 22:10-21

WHAT DO YOU DO WITH A VISION?

LEARNING MENU

Remember that persons have different learning styles: visual, oral, sensory, and so forth. Activities that accompany each Dimension in the study book offer several ways of helping learners experience growth through Bible study. Choose a variety of activities that will meet these different learning styles within your class. Be sure to select at least one activity from each of the three Dimensions.

Due to the complex nature of the Book of Revelation, some of the questions given in the study book have additional discussion material in the leader's guide. If an image or idea engages your class, continue with this discussion by using the additional information provided. Also on occasion a learning option in the following Dimensions will act as a continuation of the idea first addressed in the study book questions.

Dimension 1:
What Does the Bible Say?

(A) Answer the study book questions.

The best procedure is for the participants to work on the questions in advance of the class to allow time for study and reflection.

If this is not possible, use the questions as discussion starters either with the entire group or after dividing into smaller groups. Some possible responses to the study book questions are as follows:

1. John's time references
—are mistaken, in which case the book itself should probably be dismissed.
—are correct, but John was seeing the far-distant future. In this case what value did the book have for the original readers and everyone prior to those long-foreseen events?
—are correct, but they have a meaning beyond purely the temporal or chronological; they operate in another frame of reference.
Other options may be developed by the participants.

2. The use of *like*, *as*, and other images reveal John's struggle to convey in language an experience that transcends language. Note that the images depict rather than describe; they are fluid, not fixed. All this suggests that the vision reality is much too solid to be contained by frail human language.

Additional discussion: Use a concordance to look at all uses of *like* and *as* in Revelation. Note their use especially with reference to the images, symbols, and sounds. See if a pattern emerges.

3. Regarding Jesus' opening affirmation (1:18), if John is being given a glimpse into the profound realities of God's purposes in Christ, then something of radical significance took place in the death and resurrection of Jesus. Humanity can be liberated from its destructive bondage to brokenness

and sin (imaged as Fallen Babylon in John's vision) and be formed into a new community of healing and wholeness (imaged as New Jerusalem).

4. An angel, who in both chapters 1 and 22 is clearly Jesus, is God's agent of the revelation. Who is Jesus' "angel"? It seems most likely that Jesus was referring to what the Old Testament spoke of as the "angel of the presence" of the LORD. The "angel" is the presence of Christ. Many of the angels that play focal roles in the vision are representations of Christ.

(B) Share perceptions about Revelation.

The Book of the Revelation to John has challenged scholars and people of faith since its beginning. Your class members will have different understandings of this final book of the Bible. Be ready to facilitate different views. In advance read the synopsis of the four basic approaches described in Additional Bible Helps, page 7.

Prior to class time photocopy this information from the Additional Bible Helps to distribute to the small groups.

- Have the participants break into four groups. Give each group a copy of one of the basic approaches to Revelation.
- Allow five to ten minutes for the groups to read the information found in the Additional Bible Helps and to discuss its implications.
- Ask each group to present and defend its approach.
- Engage the large group in a discussion of how the material in the study book challenged or confirmed preconceptions about Revelation. Ask:
—Have any new possibilities of understanding opened up for you?

Suggest that the group develop a "covenant of deferred judgment" until the end of the study. Such a covenant would not require persons to abandon their understanding of Revelation, but simply commit them not to hold up their understanding as the "norm" for all class members. Such a covenant would provide a fertile ground for growth in everyone's understanding and help remove the potential for controversy and conflict that often emerges around Revelation.

Dimension 2:
What Does the Bible Mean?

(C) Compare the structure of Revelation 1 and Revelation 22:6-21.

- For this learning option you will need large sheets of paper, markers, and tape or chalkboard and chalk.
- Work together as a whole class to discern the connections between John's introductory and concluding sections of the vision. Write the findings on the chalkboard or on the paper for all to see.
- Have the participants list all the parallel terms, phrases, and themes found in 1:1-20 and 22:6-21, such as "show his servants" (1:1; 22:6); the sending of an angel (1:1; 22:6, 16); "what must soon take place" (1:1; 22:6); and the others.
- Discuss the significance of these parallels. Information in the study book (pages 8-10) may be helpful as starter ideas.

(D) Study the structure of Revelation.

- Prepare an overhead or a large paper chart of the structure of Revelation (see the article at the end of the leader's guide, "The Structure of Revelation," pages 71-72). Before class time read the article and be prepared to share this information with your class members.
- A major feature of this structure is the "core" of heavenly vision. Ask class members to read aloud the beginning statements in each section (4:1; 11:19; and 19:11). Help them to note the increasing "openness" as one moves through the vision. First, a door in heaven opened (4:1); then the temple in heaven opened (11:19); finally all of heaven opened (19:11). It is as if the vision moves John into greater and greater dimensions of the "Revelation of Jesus Christ."

Part One:
- Divide your class members into two groups. Ask the two groups to study one of the pairs of sevens in the structure of Revelation.
—**Group One**—Seven Churches (2:1-3; 3:22), Seven Seals (6:1–8:5)
—**Group Two**—Seven Trumpets (8:6–11:18), Seven Bowls (15:5–16:21)
- Have them note and then share with the other class members any similarities they find.

Part Two:
- Then ask class members to examine the introductions to the vision of the whore (17:1-3) and the vision of the bride (21:9-10).
- Discuss the similarities and differences between the two introductions.
- Have the class members then examine the conclusions to the two visions (19:9b-10; 22:6-9) and again discuss the similarities and differences. Ask:
—Why does John disobey in 22:8 the command he received in 19:10 not to worship the angel?
—What happens if we view these two events as a single situation rather than two separate ones?
—Could John be "signaling" his readers that this last portion of the vision is not to be seen sequentially but as one single vision that he has to break into three parts in order to convey?
- Remind the class that while our thought processes function sequentially and linearly, (we don't know what will come

at the end of a paragraph until we get there), visionary experience is often unitive—an instantaneous, holistic grasp of a profound and multifaceted reality.

- If possible leave up the chart on the structure of Revelation for the duration of this study. This outline will prove helpful as you continue to work your way through this complex book of the Bible.

(E) Study the vocabulary for Revelation.

Due to the complex nature of the Book of Revelation you may want to take a few minutes to focus on some of the vocabulary you will be using during this study.

- For this learning option you will need paper, pencils or pens, large sheets of paper or posterboard, markers, and tape.
- Divide your class members into three or four small groups. Provide them with paper and pens or pencils.
- Ask each small group to generate its list of vocabulary words and definitions. As resources the group may wish to use their Bibles, study books, dictionaries, Bible dictionaries, and class discussion.
- At the end of five to seven minutes, be ready to record on large sheets of paper or posterboard the words and phrases the groups have selected. Work by consensus to arrive at the definitions. As a group names a term, ask other groups if they selected this term also and what were their thoughts. Conclude with a definition that is accepted by all groups.

  Check the glossary found on page 128 of the study book for most of the central words, images, and phrases.

- If possible keep these vocabulary sheets posted. You will want to add more terms to them as you continue the study. Also some images may evolve in meaning as you get farther along in the study of Revelation. Leave space after each definition in order to add to them if appropriate.

(F) Review the seven blessings of Revelation.

- Two of Revelation's seven blessings (1:3 and 22:14) are addressed in this lesson. Both of these blessings deal with obedience to the vision. Your class might want to look ahead at the other five blessings.
- Supplies for this learning option are seven large sheets of paper or posterboards, crayons, markers, pencils, and tape.
- Divide your class members into seven groups. Assign each group a blessing. Supply each group with art supplies. Ask that each group draw a picture of what is required to receive the blessing. (Tell the class that "stick" or line people are fine—great artistic abilities are not required.)

SEVEN BLESSINGS

Revelation 1:3	Revelation 19:9
Revelation 14:13	Revelation 20:6
Revelation 16:15	Revelation 22:7
Revelation 22:14	

- After five to ten minutes ask a representative from each small group to show the group's drawing and tell of the blessing.

Dimension 3: What Does the Bible Mean to Us?

(G) Take visionary experience seriously.

- In this learning option your class members will discuss their perspectives on visionary experiences. Outline the following background information on visions to your class prior to your class discussion.

Visions are described by a wide variety of terms and phrases: mystic experiences, altered states of consciousness, awakened states of consciousness, heightened states of consciousness, and so forth. But what do these describe? Four essentials are involved in the definition of a visionary experience.

First, the experience seems to be something beyond the range of that which is usually accepted as "normal" human consciousness. Perhaps this is illustrated in Revelation when John has to turn around (1:12), to reorient himself completely, so that he might enter fully into the visionary experience that comes to him "from behind" (1:10). Paul describes this aspect of visionary experience by noting that he did not know whether he was in or out of the body (2 Corinthians 12:3).

Second, the experience seems to be one in which "normal" human consciousness is discovered to be partial and incomplete in the light of the fullness and wholeness of the visionary experience. Perhaps it was something of this reality that Paul had in mind when he said, "Now we see in a mirror, dimly, but then we will see face to face. Now I know only in part; then I will know fully" (1 Corinthians 13:12). In making a distinction among earthly human existence, Paul is touching upon the essential characteristic of visionary experience. "Normal" human consciousness is seeing in a mirror "dimly," or knowing "only in part." The visionary experience is seeing "face to face" and "knowing fully." Not that the visionary experience is opposite to normal human experience; it is, rather, the opening of normal human experience to the deeper dimensions of its own reality. Visionary experience pushes out the parameters of human perception so that the usual, limited perceptual framework is viewed in fuller, richer, and deeper meaning and purpose.

Third, visionary experience seems to be characterized by its "graced" nature. A vision is not something brought about by human effort, even though various disciplines may make one ready and receptive to visionary experiences. Such experiences come from "outside." Throughout Christian history, those who have had such experiences repeatedly describe them with such terms as being encountered, being addressed, being possessed by God. God becomes the subject of the vision and the human becomes the receiver of the vision. In Revelation, perhaps this same aspect is seen in John's falling to the ground as dead when he sees the vision and the Lord's taking control by laying his hand upon John (1:17).

Fourth, the visionary experience is holistic in nature. Visions are not simply affective, right-brained events any more than they are cognitive, left-brained events. Such experiences are both cognitive and affective, right- and left-brained, but more. They are experiences that impact the totality of the human being and go beyond the limits of human "beingness." Such experiences appear to be holistic immersions of the person involved in a larger reality of which human existence is a part.

● Following your presentation on the visionary experience, break into small conversation groups and discuss the following aspects of taking visionary experience seriously. Ask:
—Can you think of other biblical examples that follow these characteristics of visionary experiences?
● Discuss these biblical experiences in light of the information just given. Ask:
—Is it easier to read and believe these visionary experiences of our ancient biblical ancestors and early church fathers and mothers than to believe those who receive visions today? Why or why not?
—Do you think that God reveals God's self through visions to contemporary people of faith? Why or why not?
—How do you experience God's direction in your own life?

(H) Understand the final instruction.

● For this learning option you will need Bibles, paper, and pens or pencils.
● Divide your class members into small groups. Ask each group to compare Revelation 22:18-19 with Deuteronomy 4:2 and 12:32 and Proverbs 30:6.
—What was Jesus saying about the revelation?
—How does this New Testament warning compare with the Old Testament passages given? (The warning about adding or taking away from the book [Revelation 22:18-19] has often been used to attack those whose interpretations of Revelation are judged to be faulty or who have

called into question the validity of the interpretation of the ones using this text in their defense. Understanding the use of this "warning" in other biblical passages [Deuteronomy 4:2; 12:32; Proverbs 30:6], however, reveals that the issue is obedience to the word, not one of interpretation.

Rather than trying to smooth over the "roughness" of some of the things John experienced in his vision or amplifying points to make them amenable to our perspectives, the call is for us to "hear and keep" what has been conveyed to us. This instruction calls us to make our study of Revelation more than informational; it is intended to be formational for our growth to wholeness in Christ.)
● Be sure to note the importance of obedience to the word, rather than interpretation. What are your class members' responses to this concept? Ask the following questions:
—How can we be faithful by obedience to instruction that is so rich and multilayered?
—What kind of discipleship is this text calling us to?

(I) Close with a time of worship.

● Close your time together by reading responsively the "Canticle of Hope" (*The United Methodist Hymnal*, 734). You will need enough copies of the hymnal for each person to be able to read along. Recruit a class member to read aloud the light print, while the rest of the class members read the dark print. If you have someone in your class who feels comfortable teaching and leading the sung response, include this in the reading where the large, red *R* is printed.

Basic Approaches to Revelation

Scholars have developed four basic approaches to Revelation over the centuries of its interpretation. Each approach has its strengths and weaknesses. The most holistic interpretation of John's vision will seek to build upon the strengths of each approach and avoid its weaknesses.

The *preterist* approach basically understands Revelation as a document for its own day. The book is to be interpreted in the light of the sociological, political, economic, religious, and cultural conditions of the last half of the first century. While it might be possible to infer meaning from Revelation for our own day, this approach finds the primary meaning of the work in the meaning it had for the original readers. The *strength* of this approach is that it takes seriously the original context of the book. The images and symbols of the book, as well as the nature of the book itself, are to be understood within the cultural context in which they operated in the first century. This approach helps us to avoid assigning meaning to the images and symbols of Revelation that have no grounding in the original pool of images from which they were drawn. The *weakness* of this approach is that it lessens or completely removes any meaning of the book for later generations of Christians. Its basic value for the following centuries of Christians is as a witness to a particular movement within the early church.

The *historicist* approach views Revelation as a depiction of Christian or even world history from the time of Christ to the Second Coming. The approach searches the events of history for their connection with the images and flow of Revelation. Some historicists would see much of Revelation dealing with past history; others would see much of Revelation dealing with the future (this position shades over into the futurist position noted below). As one example, during the Protestant Reformation, one of the standard interpretations of the beast in Revelation 13, was that it represented the Pope who was leading the persecution of "true" Christians (i.e. Protestants). The *strength* of the historicist approach is that it recognizes the validity of John's vision for Christians of all ages, not just for the original readers. It realizes that John's vision reveals a God who acts within the flow of human history, not just at its extremes. The *weakness*, however, is that subjective and highly selective readings of history become the foundation for the understanding of the vision.

The *futurist* approach sees Revelation primarily as a vision of the last days just preceding the second coming of Christ. In a sense this approach differs slightly from the historicist position that simply limits Revelation to the last segment of history. With this method of interpretation the events of the present are carefully studied to discern situations and patterns that relate to what is taken to be preliminaries of the last days in John's vision. Of course, most futurist interpretations see some portion of Revelation related to past history, but usually no more than the first three chapters. Generally the letters to the seven churches are seen as representing seven periods of church history, with the Laodicean church usually representing the interpreter's own period just prior to the last days represented in chapters 4–22. The *strength* of this approach is that it takes seriously John's vision as it relates to God's final consummation of history. The *weakness* is that, even more than the historicist approach, this method is subjective to the extreme. In addition, the meaning of John's symbols and images are completely severed from their original sphere of meaning and the interpreter's own meanings are read into them.

The *idealist* approach presumes that behind the historically conditioned imagery of Revelation lie general spiritual principles that are valid for human existence throughout history. This approach seeks to draw out these principles and lift up their relevance for human existence in any period of history. The *strength* of this approach is that it takes seriously the validity of John's vision for times and places other than those of the original readers. It also recognizes that John's vision draws him into deeper realities that transcend the peculiarities of John's situation. The *weakness* of this method is that it tends to be the most subjective of all the approaches. All too often, the "spiritual principles" discerned in John's vision are remarkably similar to the particular perspective of the interpreter.

It seems that the best approach to John's vision is to first seek to understand it from within John's world and the pool of images he uses to convey the vision to that world. We can then begin the attempt to discern the deeper meaning of John's vision and what it means for life in Christ, first in his own day and then in each period of Christian history.

2

THE GOOD, THE BAD, AND THE UGLY (PART 1)

LEARNING MENU

Remember that persons have different learning styles: visual, oral, sensory, and so forth. Activities that accompany each Dimension in the study book offer several ways of helping learners to experience growth through Bible study. Choose a variety of activities that will meet these learning styles. Be sure to select at least one activity from each of the three Dimensions.

Dimension 1:
What Does the Bible Say?

(A) Work with the study book questions.

1. Ephesus—Cold Orthodoxy. The church in Ephesus is an example of a church with the form of godliness but without its power. It maintains the structures and practices of the faith as an end in themselves rather than a relationship of loving devotion to God.

2. Smyrna—Daring Discipleship. The church does not exist in a vacuum. When it is a vibrant witness to life in Christ, it becomes a plumb line that throws into sharp relief the bentness of the world. The greater a church's faithfulness, the greater the contrast to any bentness in the surround-

ing culture and the greater the pressure and opposition from that culture.

Additional Discussion: Can class members give contemporary illustrations of Smyrna-type churches? In what ways is your church similar to or different from the Smyrna church?

3. Pergamum—Tolerant Acceptance. One of the greatest "sins" of our day is intolerance. The golden virtue is acceptance of others, no matter how different their views or lifestyles may be. Anyone who is so intolerant as to suggest that there may be some views or lifestyles that are simply wrong is usually attacked as an intolerant bigot (receiving, often, a more intolerant treatment from the apostles of toleration than anything they have done).

Additional Discussion: The church in Pergamum is tolerant of the heresy in its midst. There are those in the church today who are intolerant of any suggestion or situation that might be different from what they are accustomed to experiencing. Ask:

—Can class members give examples of inappropriate intolerance?
—Do any of the class members see any aspects of the Pergamum syndrome (too much tolerance) in the church today?

4. Thyatira—Toleration Plus. Just as the close of each letter ("Let anyone who has an ear listen to what the Spirit is saying to the churches") draws all the churches into consideration of the faithfulness or problem of each of the other churches, so this "aside" brings every church into this situa-

tion of heresy. Could Jesus be indicating that Thyatira's attitude toward heresy is a major concern for the church?

Additional Information: Here is information to help the class understand more clearly the issue in the church at Thyatira. The Greek word for *tolerate* (NRSV) in 2:20, means "to permit," "to allow," "to condone." This needs to be understood in the light of "the rest" who do not hold with the teaching of the heresy (2:24). It would appear that the first group does not only simply tolerate the heresy, but it also affirms and supports the right of the heretics to hold the heresy even though they themselves do not participate in it.

(B) Share information about the four churches.

- Prior to class time read, then photocopy, the information in the Additional Bible Helps section of this chapter (pages 11-12) on the four ancient churches of Ephesus, Smyrna, Pergamum, and Thyatira. Also for this learning option you will need four large sheets of paper or four posterboards, markers, and tape.
- Divide your class members into four groups. Assign each group one of the four churches to research.
- Provide reference materials such as photocopied information, Bible dictionaries, or a commentary on Revelation. Ask each small group to research its church. It is helpful to know as much as possible about the historical, political, economic, and sociological setting of the churches in order to understand more fully the thrust of the letters. Give each small group one of the large pieces of paper or posterboards on which to record its findings.
- Ask a representative from each group to share the group's findings with the whole class. Post each group's printed information so that all can see and make reference to them for the next two lessons.

Dimension 2: What Does the Bible Mean?

(C) Study the theme of conquering.

- Ask your class members to divide into trios for this learning option. Using a concordance, list each use of the word *conquering* in Revelation. Ask each trio to look up one or more of these references.
- After your small groups have had a chance to look up these references, share the following information with the whole class. As each trio's reference is noted, ask for additional insights and ideas.

  "Conquering" is a focal theme throughout John's vision. The promise to the one who *conquers* is present in each of the seven letters: the Lamb has *conquered* (3:21; 5:5) and goes forth *conquering* (6:2); the faithful *conquer* Satan by

the blood of the Lamb and their witness (12:11); those who have *conquered* the beast are seen standing upon the sea mingled with fire (15:2); the Lamb will conquer the forces of the beast (17:14); and the *conqueror* will have God as God and will be God's child (21:7). In only two places is *conquering* used of the fallen order: the beast makes war against God's two witnesses and *conquers* them (11:7), and the beast is allowed to make war against the saints and to *conquer* them (13:7).

- Conclude your class discussion with the following information:

  In the context of the letters, *conquering* seems to be the consistent discipleship of living as a faithful citizen of New Jerusalem. Conquering in 12:11 and 15:2 reveals the object that is overcome: Satan and the beast, the incarnation of Satan (13:2). Satan/the beast is incarnate in the dynamics of a framework and lifestyle in total rebellion against God. This framework and lifestyle shapes the citizenship of Fallen Babylon.

  Conquering, therefore, can only take place in the midst of Fallen Babylon. Conquering is living fully as a citizen of New Jerusalem unencumbered by the bondages of Fallen Babylon though not removed from its sphere of activity. In brief, conquering is having one's life consistently shaped by the values and dynamics of New Jerusalem. This seems to be something of what Wesley and the early Methodists understood by "entire sanctification."

(D) Depict the series of seven.

There are four series of sevens in the Book of Revelation. This lesson begins study of the first of these sevens.

- For this learning option you will need large sheets of paper or large sheets of posterboard, construction paper, glue, markers, crayons, scissors, magazines, and tape.
- Divide your class members into four groups. Assign each small group one of the series of seven.
- Ask each group to read the Scripture passage, then depict in art its assigned series of seven. The groups can choose a variety of ways to represent their Scripture passage.

SERIES OF SEVENS
Seven letters—Revelation 2:1–3:22
Seven seals—Revelation 6:1–8:5
Seven trumpets—8:6–11:18
Seven bowls—15:5–16:21

- At the end of ten minutes, ask a representative of each group to explain the highlights of the group's passage.

(E) Compare and contrast the stylized letters.

- The letters to the ancient churches found in Revelation 2:1–3:22 are in a highly stylized form. In this learning option your class members will be comparing and contrasting these letters.

- Divide the class members into seven small groups and assign each group one of the ancient churches being studied. Distribute paper and pens or pencils to the groups. Have the following form written on the chalkboard or on large sheets of paper so that the whole class can see the information:

To the angel of the church in _____ write:

These are the words of_____
                                (attributes of Christ from chapter 1)

I know_____
                        (description of the church)

But I have this against you_____
(this form is reserved for the three churches that are a mixture of faithfulness and failure for the purpose of listing the church's problems, weaknesses, failures—omitted for Smyrna and Philadelphia, the faithful churches; in another form for Sardis and Laodicea, the apostate churches)

_____

(call for repentance—omitted, of course, for Smyrna and Philadelphia)

_____

(promises of blessing or curse)

_____

To everyone who conquers (a description of rewards to be given)

Let anyone who has an ear listen to what the Spirit is saying to the churches

(The last two parts are reversed in the letters to Ephesus, Smyrna, and Pergamum)

- Ask each small group to fill in the appropriate information for "their" ancient church.
- After the groups have finished compare and contrast their findings.

Dimension 3:
What Does the Bible Mean to Us?

(F) Write a letter to the church today.

- Have the students break into small groups and write a letter attempting to portray what they believe Jesus would say to

their church. It might help them to follow the pattern of the letters to the seven churches provided in learning option (E). Provide the form given in learning option (E) if you did not previously select that learning option.

(G) Contemplate the Ephesian-like church.

- If your class members have not already done so, take a few minutes to read about the church at Ephesus in the study book on page 16.
- Ask a class member to read aloud the passages from the Book of Acts listed below. Also share the summary statements below.
  The Ephesian church appears to be a church closed in upon its orthodoxy. It has lost:
—that love that once thrust it out into the world of Ephesus with such dynamic power that its leaders were hauled before an unscheduled meeting of the citizenship because of the impact they were having upon the economic and religious life of the city (Acts 19:11-41);
—that love that once made it a center from which the good news of a radical new order of being went throughout all the province of Asia (Acts 19:10);
—the offensive of love and replaced it with the defensive of orthodoxy.
- As the Book of Acts relates, the church at Ephesus was once a strong and vibrant community of believers. Yet in the Book of Revelation we read of a community that has become closed in upon its own orthodoxy.
- Discuss with your class members the following questions:
—Do you think it is easy or difficult to become self-focused on one's own orthodoxy?
—Can you note other examples from church history that would echo this self-focus?
—Where do you think our own denomination stands in comparison with the church at Ephesus?
—Is your own congregation like the church at Ephesus? If so, how?

(H) Find the balance.

- Present the following information to the class members:
  Part of our responsibility as Christians is to reach out into the world and spread the love of Christ. We share the struggle that the churches of Pergamum, Thyatira, and Ephesus had with brothers and sisters of the faith.
  Jesus gives time for repentance (2:21). The church of Thyatira also gives this woman and her followers time, but apparently their "time" has lost sight of its purpose to lead to repentance.
  These circumstances are the problem of the Thyatira-type church. When does "time for repentance" slip over into toleration of apostasy (an abandonment of one's religious faith)? The church finds it easier to condemn and

expel the wrong-doer, like the Ephesian-type church would do. The church also finds it easier to be "long-suffering" and give the wrong-doer so much "time" that it becomes tolerant of evil in its midst like the Pergamum- and Thyatira-type churches.

- Facilitate a general discussion beginning with these questions:

—Where do you see examples in your congregation of the above characteristics? (Waiting too long for change in a person's faith behavior, or not being patient enough for change to occur in a person's life under the influence of your faith community . . .)

—As a community of faith how can we know what the balance is between the appropiate length of "time for repentance" and too much time?

—How can we as a church of the nineties be open and nurturing to newcomers or people returning to the church, giving them time to discover and sort out their own faith questions, and still call them to church disciplines?

(I) Discuss the values, structures, and dynamics of culture.

Today, the *values*, *structures*, and *dynamics* of culture pressure and seek to shape the church continuously. Ask a class member to read aloud from the study book on pages 21-22, "Possibilities for the Church in Every Age."

- Discuss as a whole class the values, structures, and dynamics given in the study book. The following questions may be helpful in beginning the discussion:

—How do you see these dynamics at work in your community and church?

—How can your congregation stand against these pressures?

—In the midst of these cultural pressures, where do you see the call of your congregation?

—What is the quality of your "New Jerusalem citizenship in the midst of Fallen Babylon"?

- Close your session with a prayer for strength to be the servants of Christ in the midst of our world.

NOTE: The Dimension 4 suggested daily readings in the study book are intentionally the same for chapters 2 and 3.

Additional Bible Helps

The following information will be helpful for activity (B).

Ephesus
Ephesus (ef'uh-suhs) was one of the major cities in the Roman Empire ranking, after Rome, with Alexandria in Egypt and Antioch in Syria. It was the largest and most important seaport in the Roman province of Asia and, therefore, a major commercial center for overland trade to the

East and shipping to the entire Mediterranean area.

Ephesus was one of the cultural centers of the Roman world. As a major educational center it possessed a large library as well as numerous smaller libraries, and had a magnificent theater that seated about 24,000 people.

From antiquity, Ephesus had been the center for the worship of a mother goddess, whom the Greeks had identified as Artemis (ahr'tuh-mis) and the Romans as Diana, her huge and magnificent temple being one of the seven wonders of the ancient world. In 29 B.C. her temple was also dedicated to Roma, the "spirit" of Rome, and thus became associated with the Roman imperial cult. Ephesus was a center for the worship of the Roman emperor.

Smyrna
The history of Smyrna (smuhr'nuh) goes back into the second millennium B.C., when it was founded by the Aeolian Greeks and continues down to the present time (modern Izmir). There was one period, however, when Smyrna was "dead." About 600 B.C., Smyrna was destroyed by the king of Lydia and remained desolate for three centuries. It "came to life" when Lysimachus (li-sim'uh-kuhs) refounded it in 290 B.C. In the first century it was one of the largest and busiest commercial centers in the Roman province of Asia, vying with Ephesus and Pergamum for leadership in the province.

Situated about thirty-five miles north on the road from Ephesus, Smyrna was the center of a fertile and productive area and was further enhanced in its economic strength by its location on one of the major routes of trade to the east and China. Its large harbor enabled Smyrna to conduct a shipping trade in the Mediterranean second only to Ephesus.

Smyrna was a center for the worship of Cybele (sib'uh-lee), another of the pantheon of Greek gods and goddesses whose temples populated the Roman world. The temple of Cybele was at the shore of the Aegean, where Smyrna's "Golden Street" began. Along the street were temples to Apollo, Aesculapius, and Aphrodite. Where the street ended at the foothills, there was a magnificent temple to Zeus.

Like Ephesus, Smyrna was shaped by the economics, politics, culture, education, and religions of the Roman world. It was a large and beautiful city that possessed a famous stadium, a library, and the largest public theater in the province of Asia. Its claim as the birthplace of Homer assured its importance in education, since the works of Homer were the standard textbooks of the educational system.

Smyrna had a large Jewish population that appears to have maintained an intense hostility to the Christian community over a long period. In the letter to Smyrna, we see the hostility of the Jewish synagogue (2:9).

Why do the Jews side with the Roman political authorities against the Christians? The Jews possessed the privilege of being a licit religion in the Roman Empire. They were allowed to conduct their lives according to their own values, principles, and structures; to have their own places of worship; to be exempt from participating in the religious practices of the Empire and city; to be a "different" people in the midst of the Roman world. This toleration of Rome, however, had its limits. Whenever the Jewish community overstepped its bounds, either by causing disturbances to the status quo of the locality of which it was a part, or drawing Roman citizens into its way of life and worship (proselytizing), then Rome put its foot down.

Imagine the situation as Christians are expelled from the synagogue. (We repeatedly read in the New Testament that Paul and other early Christians began their ministries in the Jewish synagogues.) As far as the Jews were concerned the Christians were heretics, people who no longer had any part in the covenant community of God's people. As far as the Romans were concerned they were simply another sect of the Jews. Here is the problem for the Jews. They have expelled the Christians from their community and no longer have any control over them. The Christians are now out in the larger population of the city evangelizing the Gentiles with great success. Should the successful proselytizing of the Christians attract the attention of the authorities, the Jewish community may be implicated in the affair and lose their coveted privileges. To forestall this possibility, the Jews take the initiative and go themselves to the authorities to lodge complaints against the Christians. In doing so, the Jews seek to make it clear to the Roman authorities that they are abiding within the limits of their special privileges and are in no way involved in the activities of the Christians.

This would appear to be what has happened in Smyrna. The Jewish community has expelled the Christians, disclaimed any connection with them, and enlisted the aid of the local authorities against the church. This is why Jesus describes them as a synagogue of Satan. For John, the Roman power structure represented Satan/the beast/Fallen Babylon in his own day. By enlisting the aid of the Roman officials, the Jews ally themselves with "Satan" (or Rome), thus becoming an instrument of Rome's power against the church. They become a "synagogue of Satan."

Pergamum

The Romans made Pergamum the capital of the province of Asia, an honor it retained until A.D. 130. As the capital, Pergamum was blessed with the economic benefits that resulted from such a presence.

There were many temples to a wide variety of gods and goddesses in Pergamum, but three stand out as being most significant. Pergamum was the site of one of the leading centers for the worship of Aesculapius, the god of healing. The temples of Aesculapius were the hospitals of the Roman world, and the sick flocked to their precincts seeking healing. The priests of Aesculapius were skilled in the medical arts, in herbal remedies, and in forms of psychotherapy that were often very successful.

The second significant religious site in Pergamum was the altar of Zeus located at the pinnacle of the acropolis just below the temple of Athena. This magnificent altar was one of the major centers for the worship of Zeus in the Roman world.

The third important religious site was the temple dedicated to the emperor. In 29 B.C., Pergamum became the first city in the East to be given permission to build a temple for the worship of a living emperor. Augustus allowed the building of a temple to "the divine Augustus and the goddess Roma." As the capital of a Roman province, the other gods and goddesses of the Roman world were well represented and worshiped.

Pergamum was a microcosm of the religious forces of the Roman world. In every respect, Pergamum would have presented the fulness of the Roman culture and life in the first century. Here, perhaps more than in any of the other six cities, the dynamics of Fallen Babylon would have reigned supreme.

Thyatira

Thyatira (thi'uh-ti'ruh) fell under Roman control in 190 B.C. as Rome made its initial thrust into Asia Minor. It was first placed under the kingdom of Pergamum, which was allied with Rome. Subsequently, Thyatira became part of the Roman province of Asia and quickly became the chief city of the Lycus valley, noted for its trade and industry.

Located on the overland trade routes from the Mediterranean to the East, Thyatira benefited as a trans-shipment center for goods flowing both ways. Its location also gave it easy access to the markets of the Roman world for its own goods. Inscriptions reveal that a large number of local industries with strong labor guilds conducted business in Thyatira: bronze workers, coppersmiths, tanners, leatherworkers, dyers, wool workers, linen workers, patters, bakers, and slave-dealers. Lydia, the businesswoman in the purple goods worn only by the elite, who became a Christian in Philippi, was from Thyatira (Acts 16:14).

Each guild had its own deity whose worship was an integral part of membership in the guild. This resulted in a number of deities having centers of worship in Thyatira. Thyatira was also a center for the worship of Apollo, the sun god. The tendency of the ancient times was to often combine different religious beliefs into one belief. Therefore, in the absence of a temple to the emperor, Apollo had come to be equated with the emperor so that both the emperor and Apollo together were worshiped as the sons of Zeus. The worship of Artemis, while not as focal as in Ephesus, was prevalent.

Thyatira was of minor political importance in the province of Asia, so the Roman presence there would have been limited to the officials who oversaw the collection of taxes and duties on the trade goods that flowed through the city. It was in the economic and religious areas where Thyatira would have presented to the Christian community strong dynamics of the Roman world.

3

**Revelation
2:1–3:22**

$\mathcal{T}$HE GOOD,
THE BAD,
AND THE UGLY
(PART 2)

LEARNING MENU

Remember that persons have different learning styles: visual, oral, sensory, and so forth. Activities that accompany each Dimension in the study book offer several ways of helping learners to experience growth through Bible study. Choose a variety of activities that will meet these learning styles. Be sure to select at least one activity from each of the three Dimensions.

Dimension 1:
What Does the Bible Say?

(A) Work with the study book questions.

1. Clothing can tell a lot about a person. The use of clothing images is an important feature of John's vision. Help the class see that John's image relates to the integrity of one's being in relationship to Christ and to the manifestation of that quality in daily life.

2. An attribute of the church at Philadelphia shows the power of poverty. The values that shape the Philadelphia-type church simply "do not compute" in the context of the world's standards of value and worth. The church in Philadelphia puts the "success syndrome" in a whole new light.

Additional Discussion: Have the class discuss the insidious and destructive aspects of the drive for success as manifest in our culture.

3. The seven churches together form a "continuum" from faithful discipleship as citizens of New Jerusalem to abject accommodation to the values and perspectives of Fallen Babylon.

Additional Discussion: The class might make a chart of this continuum and rank the seven churches across it. Under each of the seven churches, list contemporary attributes of that type of church.

(B) Share information about the churches.

- (Note that in chapter 2, a similar exercise on the four ancient churches discussed in Revelation 2 was offered. This learning option will make a good continuation of gathering this important historical information.)
- Prior to class time read, then photocopy, the section in the Additional Bible Helps (pages 17-18) on the three ancient churches of Sardis, Philadelphia, and Laodicea. Also for this learning option you will need three large sheets of paper or posterboard, markers, and tape.
- Divide your class members into three groups; each group will research one of the ancient churches.
- Provide reference materials such as photocopied information from the Additional Bible Helps, Bible dictionaries, or a commentary on Revelation. Ask each small group to

research its assigned church. It is helpful to know as much as possible about the historical, political, economic, and sociological setting of the churches in order to understand more fully the thrust of the letters. Give each small group one of the pieces of paper or posterboard on which to record its findings.

● Ask a representative from each group to share the group's findings with the whole class. Post each group's written information so that all can see and make reference to it.

Dimension 2: What Does the Bible Mean?

(C) What are your "clothes"?

● This learning option has two parts. For **Part One** you will need magazines, large sheets of paper, glue, scissors, markers, and tape. For **Part Two** you will need paper, pencils or pens, concordances, and Bible dictionaries (look under "dress").

Part One

● Divide your class members into small groups. Equip each group with the above-mentioned supplies. Instruct each group to prepare a section of a collage on clothing.

● Then discuss the pictures of people in various styles and quality of clothing. Discuss the impressions the participants have as they look at these pictures. What kinds of "signals" do our clothes send to those around us?

Part Two

● Do a concordance study on "clothes" (3:4) and "robes" (3:18).

● The image of "clothes" plays an important role in the vision. You may find that in the Roman-Hellenistic world in general, as well as in the Old Testament, the type of clothing one wore was indicative of that person's occupation or position in society. This perceptual framework carried over into humanity's relationship with God.

● Divide your class members into two groups. Supply each group with the above-mentioned research materials for Part Two. Share the following information with each group; then allow them time to do additional research.

● **Group One:**
When Jacob purifies his family at Bethel, he orders them not only to "put away the foreign gods that are among you" but also to "change your clothes" (Genesis 35:2). Before Aaron enters the holy place, he is to wash his body and put on "the holy linen tunic, . . . the linen undergarments . . . the linen sash, and wear the linen turban, these are the holy vestments" (Leviticus 16:4). When he leaves the holy place, he removes the holy vestments and puts on his own clothes (Leviticus 16:23).

● **Group Two:**
This metaphorical use of clothing is found several times in the New Testament. Paul exhorts the Romans to "put on the Lord Jesus Christ, and make no provision for the flesh, to gratify its desires" (Romans 13:14), and reminds the Galatians, "As many of you as were baptized into Christ have clothed yourselves with Christ" (Galatians 3:27). In a more specific image, Paul reminds the Ephesians that they have been taught "to put away your former way of life, your old self, corrupt and deluded by its lusts, . . . and to clothe yourselves with the new self, created according to the likeness of God in true righteousness and holiness" (Ephesians 4:22, 24). In a similar vein he tells the Colossians, "You have stripped off the old self with its practices and have clothed yourselves with the new self, which is being renewed in knowledge according to the image of its creator" (Colossians 3:9-10), and then exhorts them "as God's chosen ones, holy and beloved, clothe yourselves with compassion, kindness, humility, meekness, and patience" forbearing one another (Colossians 3:12-13).

● Ask each group to begin their research by addressing these questions:
—How is the term *clothing* used in the passages your group has been assigned?
—Can you find other examples of similar uses of *clothing* or *being clothed*?
—How does looking at *clothing* metaphorically broaden and enrich these passages?

● Ask a representative from each group to share its findings.

● Conclude with these references in Revelation. These above examples illustrate the frame of reference within which the image of "clothes" and "being clothed" would have operated for the readers of John's vision. As the Christians of Sardis and the other churches encountered the deeper dimensions of the vision, the full dynamics of being clothed would have become clear to them. They would realize that the white garments are the "beings" of those who are being conformed to the image of God. They would realize that the change of garments comes about through the blood of the Lamb (7:14), the same blood that freed them from their sins (1:5), purchased them for God as a kingdom of priests (5:10), and the same blood by which they overcome the power of Satan in their lives (12:11). They would also see, in imagery exactly like that of the letter to Sardis, that those with this new clothing in Christ must be awake (compare 3:2) and keeping their garment, lest Jesus come like a thief (compare 3:3) and they be found naked with their shame exposed (16:15; compare 3:17-18).

(D) Research the requirements for inclusion in the book of life.

● Have the class members look at the biblical references for "the book of life." By using a concordance find when the phrase *book of life* first began to be written down in the Bible.

- As one class member reads the references from the concordance, have other class members look up the references in the Bible and read these verses aloud.
- The following material may help focus the discussion:

The deeper dimensions of "the book of life" are developed in the vision. The beast is given authority over "every tribe and people and language and nation" and "all the inhabitants of the earth" (both designate the citizenship of Fallen Babylon). These "whose name has not been written . . . in the book of life of the Lamb" (13:7-8) will worship the beast. In 17:8, the name of the inhabitants of the earth is not written in the book of life from the foundation of the world. In both places, while portraying the plurality of the citizenship of Fallen Babylon, the term for *name* in the Greek is singular. It seems John is seeing that the essence or nature of the being ("name") of citizens of Fallen Babylon has had absolutely no place in God's realm from the very beginning.

"The book of life" is the citizenship roll of New Jerusalem, the list of those whose "name" (the nature of Christ) is what God's realm has been all about from the beginning. This is confirmed in 20:12, 15, where the book of life appears in the Judgment, and anyone whose name does not appear written there is thrown into the lake of fire with all the other representatives of the fallen order (the beast and false prophet, 19:20; Satan, 20:10; Death and Hades, 20:14). In 21:27, nothing unclean can enter New Jerusalem, but only those who are written in the Lamb's book of life. That which is inconsistent with the image of Christ cannot be a part of God's realm.

(E) Who's got the keys?

- Since most of the attributes of Jesus in the letters to the churches are drawn from the vision of Jesus in chapter 1, have the class discuss the relationship between the "key of David" in 3:7, and "the keys of Death and of Hades" in 1:18.
- Ask two class members to read aloud verses 1:18 and 3:7. Then ask the class members for ideas regarding the relationship, if any, between these two key references. If a commentary on Revelation is available, read the material on these two passages.
- Include the following information in the discussion:

There may be a relationship between the "key of David" in Jesus' attributes (3:7) and the "keys of Death and of Hades" in John's vision (1:18). The readings in early manuscripts indicate that the early church understood the key of David to be closely related to the keys of Death and Hades. The image originates in Isaiah: "I will place on his shoulder the key of the house of David; he shall open, and no one shall shut; and he shall shut, and no one shall open" (Isaiah 22:22). This reference is to God's

rejection of the self-serving Shebna as steward over the house of David during Hezekiah's reign, and his replacement by Eliakim.

As the larger vision of Revelation shows, Jesus is the "Root of David" (5:5) and "the root and the descendant of David" (22:16). Obviously the image refers to Jesus' role as Davidic messiah. But a new dimension is introduced here. Jesus is not only the Davidic messiah who now rules over the promised Kingdom, he is also the steward of that Kingdom who gives or denies access into the presence of the King. By this image the vision expresses Jesus' words in the Gospel of John, "No one comes to the Father except through me" (John 14:6), and the claim of Peter and John, "There is no other name under heaven . . . by which we must be saved" (Acts 4:12).

Dimension 3:
What Does the Bible Mean to Us?

(F) Things are not always as they seem.

- For this learning option you will need paper and pens or pencils. Distribute these to each class member.
- If you have not already done so, read aloud the section on the Laodicea community found in the Additional Bible Helps on pages 17-18. Then ask a class member to read aloud Revelation 3:14-22. This passage of Scripture addresses the Laodicean church. Discuss this question:
—What is the difference between Jesus' evaluation of the Laodicean church and their own self-evaluation?
- After this discussion ask half of the class to write an evaluation of their own church. Have the other half describe how they think Jesus might evaluate it. Be sure to include contemporary issues. Compare the two evaluations (and spend the rest of the session putting out the fires!).

(G) What is Jesus' word to the church today?

- Have the students break into two groups.
- Have one group write a letter attempting to portray what they believe Jesus would say to a "good" church today, and the other group what Jesus would say to a "bad" church. Again it might help them to follow the "pattern" of the letters to the seven churches provided in chapter 2 in the leader's guide on page 10.

The "prosperity gospel" says that if we have faith and trust God, we will have prosperity and need nothing.
- Have the class discuss how the letter to Laodicea challenges this perspective. It might help to have the class contrast Laodicea with the faithful and trusting church in Smyrna.
- Ask class members if they can think of twentieth-century

examples of how Christian communities have stood against culture.

(H) Intertwine the tension of two worlds.

● Prior to class time read in the Additional Bible Helps "A Man in Two Worlds." This article discusses how John intertwines his earthly frame of reference with his spiritual frame of reference. We, too, are in two worlds.
● Highlight the information in the article about John for your class members.
● Discuss how we as contemporary Christians are of two worlds.

(I) Prepare a closing worship.

● Prepare a worship center in your classroom. This might consist of a tablecloth covering a small table with a cross on the table. Also include in this worship center white stones. Bring enough stones for each person to take one home. (You can purchase these stones from a nursery.)
● Read aloud Revelation 2:17.
● Share the following information about the image of stone and how it was understood in the ancient world.

    The term *stone* (2:17) was used in the Roman-Hellenistic world for a "ballot." One's name had to be inscribed on the citizenship lists of the city in order to be a legitimate citizen and eligible to cast ballots. The faithful are those whose names are written in the Lamb's book of life (3:5; 13:8), the citizenship ledger of New Jerusalem. Jesus is indicating that the ones who are in the process of conquering are citizens of God's new order of being, New Jerusalem. In Pergamum where Roman citizenship was so significant, Christians would have found this image forceful.
● Allow some quiet time for reflection. Lead the class in singing "Amazing Grace" (*The United Methodist Hymnal*, 378). During the singing of the hymn, invite class members to get a stone. Ask them to let this stone serve as a reminder of God's grace and promise.

Additional Bible Helps

Activity (B) in chapter 4 involves learning more about other visions of God. Reading selections in *Classics of Western Spirituality* (Paulist Press) by any interested students prior to the next class meeting could include the following: "Julian of Norwich," pages 1-39; "Teresa of Avila," preface and introduction; and "Hildegard of Bingein," pages 1-22, 26-35, and 59-61. This multi-volume series is out of print but is likely available in a public or church library.

A Man in Two Worlds

John's personal introduction (1:9-11) focuses upon one of the major dynamics of the entire vision. John inseparably intertwines his earthly, historical frame of reference ("I . . . was on the island called Patmos . . .") and his spiritual frame of reference ("I was in the Spirit on the Lord's day . . ."). After the vision of Christ (1:12-16), he is told to convey the vision of the spiritual frame of reference to the seven earthly, historical churches of Asia (1:17-20), which are thoroughly immersed in the brokenness of their Fallen Babylon world. The vision is not simply some otherworldly, privatized spiritual experience of John's, unconnected to the problems of daily life in the world; it is a vision for the citizens of New Jerusalem as they live out their discipleship in the midst of Fallen Babylon.

    Not only is John a brother of the Christian communities with which he is sharing his vision (1:9a), he is also a coparticipant with them "in the persecution and the kingdom and the patient endurance" in Jesus. These characteristics describe the experience of the citizens of New Jerusalem (the Kingdom) as they live lives of faithful discipleship (patient endurance) in the midst of Fallen Babylon's pressures and persecutions (persecution).

    John's location in the world of his readers not only places him geographically (1:9b), it also reveals the depth of his participation in the "persecution and kingdom and patient endurance." His faithful discipleship had resulted in his being banished or exiled to the island of Patmos. This bare, rocky, volcanic island was located in the Aegean about forty miles southwest of Miletus. It was about ten miles long and five miles wide, rising to an elevation of about a thousand feet. Such desolate, barren islands were frequently used by the Roman government as places of exile or banishment. John's banishment was "because of the word of God and the testimony of Jesus." This phrase describes Christian life in the world as faithful obedience to the will of God, which manifests forth in the world the image of Jesus. John was banished to Patmos because his New Jerusalem citizenship was too radical a challenge to the values, structures, and dynamics of Fallen Babylon as embodied in the Roman world.

    John then gives his spiritual location (1:10a): "I was in the spirit on the Lord's day." John emphasizes his simultaneous participation in two worlds by using the same word he used to describe his location on Patmos. He is at one and the same time fully involved with Christian discipleship in the world and fully immersed in the Spirit.

    The phrase, "in the spirit," is found throughout the New Testament to describe the Christian's life in relationship with God. Jude exhorts his readers to "pray in the Holy Spirit" (Jude 20); in a puzzling passage, Peter tells his readers that the gospel was preached to the dead, "though they had been judged in the flesh as everyone is judged, they might live in the spirit as God does" (1 Peter 4:6); Paul reminds the Philippians that they are the true circumcision "who worship in the Spirit of God" (Philippians 3:3), and, like Jude, tells the Ephesians to "pray in the Spirit at all times" (Ephesians 6:18); Paul exhorts the Galatians, "If we live by the Spirit, let us also be guided by the Spirit" (Galatians 5:25). His definitive statement is, "You are not in the flesh; you are in the Spirit, since the Spirit of God dwells in you" (Romans 8:9). Paul had just contrasted two orders of being: those "according to the flesh" and those "according to the Spirit" (Romans 8:5-8). Paul describes the role of the Holy Spirit in revealing the deep things of God to those who love God (1 Corinthians 2:9-12).

Therefore, to be "in the Spirit" is both the normal condition of Christian life and, at the same time, the opening to visionary experience. To be "in the Spirit" is to experience life in a new order of being, to have one's life shaped by values, structures, and dynamics that are in radical contrast to those of the world. It certainly seems reasonable, therefore, to presume that being "in the Spirit" opens one to the possibility of being drawn into deeper visionary experiences. This is what happens to John. He is "in the Spirit," and then experiences the approach of God, which opens to him far deeper dimensions of that realm of being. John is a man powerfully and transformationally living in two worlds.

Sardis

The importance and power of Sardis lay in its location on the major corridor from the Aegean into the Anatolian plateau to the east. Sardis controlled the route to and from the east as well as the north-south route from Pergamum. Both politically and commercially Sardis possessed a vital location, and the succession of ruling powers from the Lydian, Persian, Seleucid, and Pergamum kings to the Roman Empire all maintained Sardis as a major center.

Sardis had an impregnable acropolis, which was one of the sources of both its success and its failure. The impregnable fortress enabled Sardis to maintain control of the region and roads against all enemies. But twice in its history Sardis became so complacent about its impregnability that it was captured by stealth. During Cyrus's expansion of Persian control, Sardis fell when Cyrus sent a man to climb up a narrow crevice into the sleeping acropolis and open the gates to the invading army. In 218 B.C., there was a repeat performance when Antiochus sent fifteen men up the acropolis to open the gates to the invaders while the city slept.

As a center of commerce in the first century, Sardis was also a powerful economic and political center of the Roman province of Asia. This brought all the trappings of the Roman way of life to Sardis. Along with other cities of the time it boasted a theater, a stadium, and a gymnasium. It possessed a large temple of Artemis, who had been identified with the worship of the local goddess, Cybele. Cybele, the patron deity of Sardis, was believed to have the power to restore the dead to life.

Philadelphia

Philadelphia was founded to serve as an example of Greek culture in the recently annexed territories of Lydia and Phrygia and as an outpost of the Pergamene kingdom. Not too long after its founding, Philadelphia passed into Roman control in 133 B.C.

Philadelphia enjoyed three sources of prosperity: trade along the routes upon which it was located, agriculture from the fertile plains to its north (especially vineyards), and industry of textiles and leather production.

Geologically, Philadelphia was located close to the continental fault line, and thus was plagued with destructive earthquakes, as were most of the cities in the province of Asia (a factor which gives weight to the "earthquake" image of John's vision). A tremendous earthquake had devastated the area in A.D. 17. Because of the constant threat of earthquake, Philadelphia never became a large city.

As the center of a vine-growing area, the worship of Dionysus, the god of wine, was one of the major forms of religious expression. After the emperor Tiberius had provided funds for rebuilding from the earthquake of A.D. 17, Philadelphia founded a cult to Germanicus, the adopted son and heir of Tiberius. Numerous temples and religious festivals had their home in Philadelphia, including the many deities worshiped by the manufacturing guilds.

Laodicea

Laodicea prospered under Roman control, being much more suitable as a center of trade and commerce than a military site. Laodicea was one of the wealthiest cities of the province of Asia. In A.D. 60 when it was devastated by a great earthquake, the Roman government offered assistance in rebuilding. Laodicea refused and rebuilt itself in even greater glory than it had previously enjoyed. Its location on the major east-west and north-south trade routes resulted in its becoming a major banking center.

Laodicea was famous for its textile industry, especially the luxurious woolen garments and rugs made from the special black wool that had been developed through selective breeding techniques. The Laodicean textile industry exported four different kinds of outer garments and a special tunic known as the *trimita*, which was so famous that Laodicea was sometimes called Trimitaria.

In addition to its wealth and industry, Laodicea was also the home of a famous medical school associated with the temple of Men, a Carian god of healing who became associated with Aesculapius in Roman times. This school was known especially for its Phrygian powder, from which an ointment effective for certain eye diseases was made.

As with every prosperous Roman city, Laodicea offered the worship of the pantheon of Greek and Roman gods as well as a variety of ancient Phrygian deities, to say nothing of being a center of the imperial cult.

The one drawback for Laodicea was that it had no water supply of its own except for what could be transported from two nearby tributaries of the Lycus river, or from the Lycus river itself two miles away. For utility purposes, water was piped to Laodicea from the hot springs near Hieropolis about six miles away. By the time the water arrived at Laodicea it was lukewarm. It was not used for drinking, except as an emetic to cause either vomiting or movement of the bowels.

Conclusion

In each of the letters the situation of the church in some way reflects the setting in which the church is located, each, that is, except Ephesus, which had so isolated itself from the world that there is no evidence of its interaction with its culture. Smyrna and Philadelphia reflect the pressures that arose from Jewish instigation of local authorities. Pergamum and Thyatira reflect the accommodation that threatens the church from the pressures of the Roman culture of each city. Sardis, like its ancestors, is asleep in the face of the enemy. But it is the worst of the churches, Laodicea, which evidences the closest affinity to its cultural setting.

SEVEN HISTORICAL CHURCHES OF ASIA

City	Characteristics (political, geographical, or economic)	Commendation	Judgment of Churches	Key Phrase or Image
Ephesus	largest, most important seaport in Roman province of Asia	faithful church	has lost quality of Christian love; has closed in upon its own orthodoxy & shut out world	Abandoned the love you had at first (2:4)
Smyrna	major trade route to East; large seaport	I know your affliction and poverty	(none)	Be faithful unto death . . . give(n) the crown of life (2:10b)
Pergamum	wealthy city; location of many temples to wide variety of gods and goddesses	Holding fast to Christ's name in midst of culture	neither actively rejects nor accepts those who accommodate culture	image of two-edged sword (2:12); one edge-Roman power and one-edge Christ
Thyatira	strong local industries, each having its own deity	faithful church, maturing in its life and witness to Christ	actively tolerate those who accommodate culture	image of Jezebel (2:20)
Sardis	wealthy city, large-scale gold refining; controlled commerce routes East and North-South passages; well fortified city	(none)	not fulfilling their life as citizens of New Jerusalem; forgotten the Word; lost their witness	Wake-up! image of garments/ clothes (3:4)
Philadelphia	three sources of prosperity— trade routes, agriculture, textile production	Jesus indicated his solidarity with the church through self-identification as "holy"	Failure to *maintain* relationship with God results in losing what one has had in the relationship	the power of a name (3:12)
Laodicea	wealthy city—medical school; black woolen garment production; non-palatable mineral water as only close water source	(none)	church is indistinguishable from culture, rather than community shaped by image of Christ	image—water "you are . . . lukewarm . . . spit you out of my mouth (3:16)

4

Revelation 4:1–5:14

$\mathcal{D}$EEP HEAVEN

LEARNING MENU

Keep in mind your students, their needs and interests, and how they seem to learn best. Choose at least one activity from Dimensions 1, 2, and 3.

Dimension 1:
What Does the Bible Say?

(A) Work with the study book questions.

1. John's statement "at the same time I was in the spirit," indicates a continuation of the visionary experience begun in 1:10. At the close of the vision, John again notes his being in the spirit (17:3; 21:10) as an indication of the unified and holistic nature of his vision. John is not seeing separate visions; he sees one tremendous vision.

2. A way to compare John's vision of God in heaven (4:2-8) with his vision of New Jerusalem (21:10-27) would be to have one group list all the attributes of God in heaven, the other those of New Jerusalem.

Have the participants discuss particularly
(1) the twenty-four unit structure in both parts of the vision: the circle of twenty-four elders in chapter 4 and the square of twelve gates and twelve wall foundations in chapter 21;

(2) the presence of a four-part image: the four living creatures in chapter 4 and the foursquare city in chapter 21;
(3) the role of jasper in both places and (4) the image of openness (4:1 and 21:25).
Could John be describing the same reality in two different ways?

3. The significance of the scroll written on both sides and sealed with seven seals is complete completeness. The class might want to discuss 22:18-19 in light of the scroll from which nothing can be taken because of its seals and to which nothing can be added because it is totally filled with writing.

This might also be a good point to discuss the inexorable nature of God's purposes and how this relates to human free will.

Additional Information: Before class time read the Additional Bible Helps article on "The Nature of Scrolls." Incorporate information from this article in your discussion of the scroll in God's right hand.

(B) Study other visions of God.

This type of study will give a broader frame of reference for understanding John's vision.

Part One:
● Have the class study other visions of God in the Bible and through Christian history. Divide your class members into four groups. Assign the following Scripture passages or early church history people to the small groups:

Resources needed for this learning option are several Bibles and collections of early church fathers and mothers. *Classics of Western Spirituality* (Paulist Press) has text and an introduction on Julian of Norwich, Teresa of Avila, and Hildegard of Bingen. This multivolume series is now out of print but might be found in your public or church library.

Group One: Exodus 3–4; 33:17-23; Isaiah 6
Group Two: Ezekiel 10; Daniel 7:9-14
Group Three: Julian of Norwich or Hildegard of Bingen
Group Four: Teresa of Avila.
● From this study, the participants might discuss
—the nature of the visions, similarities and differences;
—the spiritual posture and situation of the person who received the vision;
—the aspects of God perceived.

Part Two:
● For this learning option you will need paper and pens or pencils for each group. Also you will need a chalkboard and chalk or large sheets of paper and markers.
● Compare John's vision of God (4:2-3, 5-8) with Ezekiel 1:4-28.
● Divide your class members into small conversation groups. Ask each group to compare the Scripture passages listed above. As they work, ask them to write down their findings.
● After the small groups have had several minutes to do their work, ask a representative from each group to serve as a spokesperson as you make a chart of Ezekiel's vision of God (Ezekiel 1:4-28) and John's vision of God (Revelation 4:2-3, 5-8).
● Using their input note all the attributes and aspects given of God in these two visions.
● Have the participants analyze the similarities and differences between the two accounts.
● One focus of this activity should be to determine what is characteristic of John's vision of God, since his experience of God shapes the entire vision.
NOTE: John does not go as far as Ezekiel in describing the appearance of God (4:2c-3). Ezekiel saw something like a human form (Ezekiel 1:26). Also review "The Throne" on page 23 in the Additional Bible Helps.

Dimension 2: What Does the Bible Mean?

(C) Discover the meaning of the term *in the spirit*.

John tells us he is "in the spirit" as he experiences his vision

(1:10). This phrase is used several times through the New Testament. In this learning option your class members will be researching the use of this phrase and finding out that this refers to the experience of being in relationship with God.
● For this learning option you will need paper, pens or pencils, Bibles, and concordances.
● Divide your class members into three or four small groups. Ask each group to look up several "in the spirit" references. (Refer them to their study books, question 1 in Dimension 1. Note that references begin after Acts 2.)
● Then have the participants discuss the New Testament experience of life "in the spirit."
NOTE: One aspect of the discussion should highlight the fact that life "in the spirit" is **not** some type of special, extraordinary experience only known by a select few. For the New Testament writers, Christian life was an experience of constant relationship with God through the Holy Spirit. This should become evident as the participants note the wide variety of life's experiences that are described as being "in the spirit" by the New Testament writers. Review "A Man in Two Worlds," pages 16- 17, for additional insights.
● Ask a representative from each group to share their findings with the whole class. Give additional information when appropriate.

(D) Consider Jesus as the door.

● Have the class look at John 10:7-10 where Jesus images himself as the "gate" of the sheep, using the same Greek term as used in Revelation 4:1 for the open door.
● If your class is large, you might want to divide into smaller conversation groups to discuss this image.
● Ask:
—Could this vision be indicating that Jesus is the "door" through which John perceives the deeper realities of heaven?
—If this is possible, could Jesus also be the open temple in 11:19, especially when God and the Lamb are the Temple of the New Jerusalem in 21:22?
—Finally, could Jesus be the open heaven in 19:11, since what is seen immediately is the victorious Christ?
—What possibilities do these ideas have for our understanding of John's vision as "The Revelation of Jesus Christ"?

(E) Study the role of the sea in John's vision.

● For this learning option you will need chalkboard and chalk or large sheets of paper and markers, and Bibles.
● Make a chart of all the uses of the word *sea* in John's vision, noting whether the use is literal, metaphorical, or possibly both. (Here are the Scripture references: 4:6; 5:13; 7:1, 2, 3; 8:8, 9; 10:2, 5, 6, 8; 12:12; 13:1; 14:7; 15:2; 16:3; 18:17, 19, 21; 20:8, 13; 21:1.)

TEACHING TIP

Discuss the general use of metaphor in literature. Here is one definition: metaphor—a figure of speech in which a term is transferred from the object it ordinarily designates to an object it may designate only by implicit comparison, example being *the evening of life*. (*The American Heritage Dictionary*, Houghton Mifflin Company, 1985; page 790)

● Discuss what John is seeing at each place where the usage is clearly metaphorical.
● Once this is done, consideration might be given to those places where the use is unclear. Ask:
—Would the same type of metaphorical use help to clarify those uncertain places?
● Finally, reconsider those uses of *sea* that were thought to be literal. Ask:
—Do any of them now have the possibility of being metaphorical?
—How does this shift the understanding of the passage?

(F) Research the role of worship in John's vision.

● For this learning option you will need 3-by-5 cards or slips of paper and pencils for every member of your class. Also you will need chalkboard and chalk or large sheets of paper and markers. Pass out the cards and pencils to each class member.

Part One:
● On these cards ask your class members to write down a definition of the word *worship*. Include in this description at least three components of worship. They need not write their names on the cards.
● Collect the cards.
● Recruit a "scribe" to record the components as they are read, making a checkmark by those items that are repeated.
● Have the class first develop its shared understanding of what worship is. While there will undoubtedly be diversity of perception as to what constitutes worship, there should also be some common core elements around which that diversity emerges. Clarify that common core.

Part Two:
● Research each mention of worship in John's vision. Terms such as *sing, worship, cry out, voices in heaven*, and *hallelujah* will lead to those sections of the vision that portray worship. In addition, the terms *blasphemy, blasphemies*, and *blaspheming* often describe the *worship* of Fallen Babylon, a negative worship of God.
● Develop a synopsis of the nature of worship as it is portrayed in John's vision.
● Ask class members to evaluate the perspective of worship with what the group found in John's vision.

● Discuss how worship in the vision constitutes the citizenship of both New Jerusalem and Fallen Babylon. (A fruitful discussion might be developed around the statement, "We become like what we worship.")
● One outcome for this process is for the participants to realize that the worship of New Jerusalem shapes its citizens into the likeness of God and the Lamb (having the "word of God and testimony of Jesus" [1:2; 1:9; 6:9]; having God's name on their forehead [7:3; 9:4; 14:1; 22:4]). By the same measure, the worship of Fallen Babylon shapes its citizens with the destructive and dehumanizing bondage of the beast and false prophet (its name on their foreheads or right hands [13:16]).

(G) Consider everything in hand.

● For this learning option you will need a concordance (two if possible), paper, pens or pencils, and Bibles.
● Divide the class into two groups.
Group One:
● Using a concordance, have this group study the uses of *right hand* in the Old Testament. (They should discover that the right hand denotes a position of preference or prestige as well as indicates the action of the person involved. Note that the term *God's right hand* often expresses the fulfillment of God's purposes in whatever situation is being dealt with.)
Group Two:
● Using a concordance, have the class members in this group study the passages in the New Testament that describe Jesus as being at God's right hand. Ask:
—While this is obviously a position of honor, could it also carry the image of Jesus as God's action?
—Might it represent Jesus as the fulfillment of God's purposes? If so, how?
● After about ten minutes ask a representative from each group to share their findings.
—How do these references of "God's right hand" differ?
—How are they similar?

(H) A picture is worth a thousand words.

● For this learning option you will need drawing paper, crayons and/or markers, tissue paper and/or construction paper, scissors, and glue.
● Ask your class members to try to draw a picture of what John saw as expressed in 4:1–5:14. (Some individuals may try to draw all the components of John's vision of the throne, while others may only want to draw one part. Allow freedom in how your class members want to participate. Remember that some adults are hesitant about displaying their drawing. Be supportive with their efforts. The class might want to attempt such a picture collectively.)
● Ask class members who feel comfortable in doing so to show their picture. Using these pictures or the class pic-

ture, focus a discussion upon the relationships between God and the Lamb, the four creatures, the twenty-four elders, and the hosts of heaven.

Dimension 3: What Does the Bible Mean to Us?

(I) Discuss the role of the scroll.

• Discuss the role of the scroll in God's right hand that only the Lamb who was slaughtered is able to open. Read aloud 4:9–5:10.
• Then ask your class members:
—Why is the image of the "slaughtered" Lamb introduced in conjunction with the opening of the scroll? (Not only is it the first characteristic of the Lamb that John sees, it is also the primary focus of the new song of the twenty-four elders [5:9-10]. It was also one of the first things Jesus said to John: "I was dead . . . ." [1:18].)
—What do you think is the significance of the image of the seven stars in Jesus' *right hand* (1:20)?
• After looking at these references, ask:
—What do you think this says to the church with respect to its role in the world?
—Does it give new dimension to the church as those who have the word of God and the testimony of Jesus?

(J) Study images of falling (bowing), worshiping, and casting the crown.

• Introduce the following concepts:
John's imagery for the deep inner relationship of the elders with God is alien to our culture. We are not a culture in which bowing is practiced nor are crowns an integral part of who we are. Worship, as may have been discovered in activity (F), also has many diverse understandings for us. In order to transfer the reality of John's images into our own relationship with God, we need images or symbols that will engender the same deep inner posture of relationship with God that John's images portray.
• Divide the large group into three smaller ones. Give each group a different topic to research.

Group One:
• Study the idea of bowing and its role in the culture of John's day. A helpful resource might be an immigrant or visitor from China, Japan, or Korea, cultures in which the meaning of bowing in John's vision is practiced.
• Develop as clear an understanding as possible for what kind of relationship with God is being portrayed through the image of bowing.
• Ask the group to develop images from their culture that would convey the same reality as John's image of bowing.

Group Two:
• Have a second group research the image of worship in the culture of the first century. The primary focus should be the Jewish tradition of the Diaspora, although Palestinian Judaism as well as the worship of the Roman religious should also be considered. Here a resource such as *Backgrounds of Early Christianity*, by Everett Ferguson (Eerdmans, 1993), will provide information on both the Jewish and Roman religious practices as well as a wealth of bibliographical information on other resources. The *Interpreter's Dictionary of the Bible* (Abingdon) also will provide this information. Look under "Dispersion."
• Ask this group to develop as complete an understanding as possible about the relationship with God that is being portrayed by John's vision of worship.
• This group should seek to find images or symbols from their own culture that depict what John is portraying.

Group Three:
• Ask the third group to research the role of the crown image in John's day. The place to start is with the Old Testament although, again, in the Roman world also the image of crown would have a powerful impact.
• This group should clarify what the image of casting the crowns before the throne of God plays in a person's relationship with God.
• Ask the group to seek images or symbols from their own culture that convey the essence of what John is seeing about relationship with God.
• After each group has done its work, come together in the large group to share findings with each other.
• Discuss the dynamics of relationship with God that John is seeing.
• "Rewrite" this portion of John's vision using imagery that presents the reality of the vision in terms that speak powerfully to our culture today.
• Remind the group that in John's vision, the elders perform these actions whenever the four living creatures give glory, honor, and thanks to God, which, as the vision makes clear, is perpetually ("day and night without ceasing," 4:8).
• Ask:
—What does this say to us with respect to our relationship with God in the midst of our daily lives?

(K) How does your church worship?

• The picture of the worship of God and the Lamb (Creator and Redeemer) in the vision provides a frame of reference by which we can assess the vitality of our own worship as a community of faith. A number of the elements of worship in the vision seem to be crucial to a dynamic and holistic worship of God.
• Ask the class to analyze the worship life of their community of faith with the following guides from John's vision:
—Does the worship exalt God as Creator in such a way that

the worshipers are acknowledging their creatureliness and their dependence upon their Creator?

—Does the worship of God as Creator result in a profound sense of responsibility and stewardship for the created order? (This stewardship, if genuine and holistic, would include the stewardship of one's own physical well-being through the avoidance of habits or lifestyles that are detrimental to good health.)

—Does the worship acclaim God as having glory, honor, and power, or does the worship subtly enlist God as the guarantor of the worshipers' glory, honor, and power? (If the worship is genuine, then it will instill humility, meekness, and gentleness in the character of the worshipers, a meekness that can stand unflinchingly against the world's powerful persuasions to manipulate, control, and abuse others.)

—Does the worship acknowledge the Lamb as the Redeemer? (Such acknowledgment will have the cross at its center as does John's vision. Here is no theoretical redemption but a radically costly redemption. Such worshipers will have a sense of their sin and brokenness.)

—Does the worship shape the community as priestly servants of God to one another and the world? (Such a community will be receptive of all since the Lamb's death can redeem people from every national group, every subculture, every language group, every people group. Such a community will be service oriented, not satisfaction oriented.)

—Does the worship increasingly shape the life of the community in their daily walk in the world?

Additional Bible Helps

The Throne

The throne image comes from the East where absolute rulers sat on thrones that represented their power and authority over the people. So close was the relationship between the ruler and the throne in the biblical perspective that the terms first become synonyms (compare 2 Samuel 3:10). Then *throne* comes to signify the rule itself as in 2 Samuel 7:16, where God says to David, "Your throne shall be established forever." This throne of David subsequently came to be associated with the throne of God and God's rule over Israel: "[God] has chosen my son Solomon to sit upon the throne of the kingdom of the LORD over Israel" (1 Chronicles 28:5). Isaiah (6:1), Ezekiel (1:26; 10:1), and Daniel (7:9) all have visions of God seated upon a throne. In the Psalms God's throne in heaven is a recurring theme (Psalms 11:4; 45:6; 93:2; 103:19).

In John's vision, with the exception of Satan's throne and the thrones of the elders and those who rule with Christ, all uses of *throne* refer to the presence of God to which everything else relates. The fullness of the spirit is before the throne (1:4). God's throne is also the Lamb's throne (3:21;

5:6; 7:17). The twenty-four elders are around the throne together with the four living creatures, the heavenly hosts, and the multitude of the redeemed. The altar for the offering of the prayers of the saints is before the throne (8:3), and the theophany (define manifestation) of God comes forth from the throne, as does the river of the water of life. God's throne is also the great white throne of judgment (20:11), before which lies the sea (4:6), which, as will be seen shortly, represents the realm of rebellion. The almost inseparable union of God and the throne forms the center of life for the entire realm that worships the One who sits upon the throne and the center of destruction for those who worship the beast.

The Breastplate

Each of the stones in the breastplate represent one of the tribes of Israel. The emerald may represent the tribe of Judah. In John's vision, the emerald rainbow seems to represent the aura of God's radiance that extends out from God's being.

There may be a double meaning in John's selection of the emerald rainbow. The rainbow, since Noah, represented the mercy of God that tempers the divine judgment. The emerald, representing the tribe of Judah, may represent the lion of the tribe of Judah (5:5), Jesus, through whom the "radiance" of God's being is made manifest (21:23) and in whom the depth of God's mercy is made known.

The Nature of Scrolls

Normally, scrolls were only written on one side so that when rolled up the writing would be protected. This scroll was totally filled up, complete, nothing could be added to it. While documents with seven seals are found from the Roman world of John's day, it is more likely that the seven seals of the vision represent the finality of the scroll. The presence of the seven seals insured that nothing could be removed from the writing. A scroll written on both sides and totally sealed is something absolutely unchangeable.

The True Worship of God

John sees that the church in its worship and praise of God becomes the structure within which God and the Lamb are enthroned. The fullness of the church is represented in the elders, just as the true nature of the church's worship is seen in the nature of the elders' worship.

The central theme of the first heavenly vision is the worship of God the Creator and of the Lamb the Redeemer. In chapter 4, after describing the heavenly throne room (4:2-8), the focus is on the worship of God as Creator by the heavenly hosts (4:9-11). In chapter 5, after describing the scroll and the Lamb (5:1-8), the focus is on the worship of the Lamb as Redeemer by the heavenly hosts and all creation (5:9-14).

5

**Revelation
6:1–8:5**

𝒯HE AGONY
AND THE ECSTASY

Dimension 1:
What Does the Bible Say?

(A) Answer the questions in the study book.

1. Most scholars believe this rider to be Christ. The first article in Additional Bible Helps could be introduced into this discussion since it highlights a number of characteristics of these riders that have wider implications in the vision.

Additional Discussion: Ask the class to compare the first rider and the rider in 19:11 (and following verses) by creating a chart of the attributes of the two riders. One outcome of this exercise should clarify the possibility of the first rider being Christ.

2. The fourth rider draws together the dynamics of the second (killing and sword) and third (famine) riders. Death and the realm of death—Hades—are portrayed as encompassing the activities of the two previous riders. The fourth

rider is the ultimate consequence of the entire rebellious order. (See page 43 in the study book.)

3. The study of the term *tribulation* may be one of the more interesting issues for your class members. When translating from one language to another, especially from an ancient language to a modern language, the nuances of a word and its original meaning are difficult to know for certain. The NRSV translates the same Greek term differently in each appearance: in 1:9—"persecution"; in 2:9-10—"affliction"; in 2:22—"distress"; and in 7:14—"ordeal." This may well indicate sensitivity to the heavy dispensational overlay that the term *tribulation* has come to denote.

One school of thought has taken this term to mean a time of intense pressure upon Christians toward the end of the world. Another school sees this as a time of great torment for unbelievers following the "rapture" of believers out of the world. A careful study of the vision, however, reveals that *tribulation* was something John was experiencing in his lifetime (1:9), something Christians were experiencing in their life in the world (2:9-10).

Tribulation describes the experience faithful citizens of New Jerusalem experience at the hands of Fallen Babylon. John is banished to Patmos because of the word of God and the testimony of Jesus (1:9) and it is one of the "good" churches, Smyrna, which is experiencing tribulation at the hands of its secular community.

Additional Discussion: Since the NRSV translates the

same Greek term differently in each appearance, try reading these passgaes and substituting the word *tribulation* for—"persecution" (1:9); "affliction" (2:9-10); "distress" (2:22); and "ordeal" (7:14). As you read these passages, think of John's use of the term as something he was experiencing in his lifetime while being a faithful follower of Christ.

Dimension 2: What Does the Bible Mean?

(B) Discuss the relevancy of John's vision.

The strange imagery of the seven seals has made it highly susceptible to equally strange interpretations. These interpretations are almost always rooted in the interpreter's larger perspective on John's vision. This is especially the case when that perspective presumes that John's vision is about the end of the world or, at least, a future far removed from John's day. In such a case, however, John's vision would have been meaningless for his original readers. Another perspective on Revelation presumes that John was writing only for his own time. In such a case, John's vision is meaningless for future readers.

● Discuss whether there may be a perspective on John's vision that makes it relevant for both his original readers as well as subsequent generations of believers. Ask class members to share their perspectives on John's vision.
● Divide your class members into small discussion groups of three or four. Ask:
—What thoughts or ideas did you bring into this study?
—Have you read the Book of Revelation before this study?
—Do you remember any sermons being preached from Revelation? If so, what do you remember?
—Do you hold a more future-oriented perspective of the material in this book? (If so, these persons may have had difficulty with the material in the study book, and it may be helpful to allow them to share their concerns.)
● It will be important for the future development of this series on Revelation to help the class at least remain open to the possibility that John's vision is neither totally past-oriented nor totally future-oriented. There needs to be some openness to the possibility that John had a vision of the deeper realities of God's presence, purpose, and action in all of human history through Christ. In such a case, John's vision was extremely relevant to the original readers but also remains vitally relevant to Christians.

(C) Illustrate the four riders.

● For this learning activity you will need five large sheets of posterboard or large sheets of paper, markers, magazines (news, business, denominational, and others), scissors, glue, and tape.
● Divide your class members into four groups. Assign each group one of the four riders.
● Ask each small group to make a collage about its rider. Try to relate the essential characteristics of each of these riders to present-day conditions. For instance, how is the destructive violence of the second rider manifest in the world today? How are the economic injustices of the third rider manifest in today's marketplace? If magazine pictures that are appropriate for the rider are not available, the group may draw pictures or write words or phrases on their paper.
● After the groups have had several minutes to work, engage the class in a discussion of the four riders. On the last piece of paper, chart the attributes of each of the riders. Ask a representative from each group to report.
● As the groups report write on the chart some contemporary illustrations of the actions of each rider. (To provide the class with starters of possible examples of how one could interpret these images, the explosion of evangelism in Africa and Korea might be an example of the "conquering" of the first rider. The present situation in Bosnia or Chechnya might well illustrate the activities of the second rider. The increasing numbers below the poverty level in the midst of America's affluence might reveal the activities of the third rider. The prevailing moral decadence—spiritual death—of Western culture might exhibit the consequences of the fourth rider.)

TEACHING TIP
The Bible often associates human spiritual qualities with colors—white with purity, black or darkness with destruction and evil. This is the case with the writer of Revelation. When teaching this material one needs to be sensitive not to correlate the biblical writer's symbolic uses of color with skin pigmentation and modern race relations.

(D) Research and reflect on the use of "white robes."

● Assemble Bibles, concordances, paper, and pens.
● Divide class members into several small groups. Be sure each group has several Bible translations, paper, pens, and access to a concordance.
● The white robe is a very significant image in the vision. Pose this question to your small groups for their research and reflection:
—What does the image of the "white robe" convey?
—Name as many as you can of the various qualities or attributes usually associated with the color white.
● Discuss which, if any, of these attributes are being employed by the vision.

—Using a concordance for Revelation, ask your small groups to make a list of who has white garments.

—In Revelation 19:8 John sees that the bright, pure linen garments of the bride are the righteous deeds of the saints. Assuming that *bright* and *pure* are synonyms for *white*, does this reveal anything to us about the white garments?

● You might also want to ask your small groups to discuss how one "soils" her garment (3:4), as well as how one makes his garment white (7:14).

● Ask:

—Does this relate in any way to the repeated description of the faithful as those who have the word of God and the testimony of Jesus? (One goal of this exercise would be to help the participants realize that the white robe represents the outer manifestation of the inner quality of being in a vital relationship with God, an image of the inseparable connection between being and doing.)

(E) Study the use of the image of 144,000.

● Ask the group, Who are the 144,000?

● Prior to the session, make a chart showing John's use of 144,000. Show how the symbol first represents the redeemed of Israel—the first covenant community of God's people. Then show that the second use of the symbol expands to include non-Jews. Since the 144,000 with the Lamb have been redeemed from "the earth" (14:3) and from "humankind" (14:4), this is an obvious reference to all of humanity and not just to Jews, even though the vision retains the first covenant images of Mount Zion and first fruit.

Finally, show that the image of 144,000 becomes "submerged," hidden in the dimensions of New Jerusalem, whose cubic dimensions are 12,000 stadia (in the Greek) on each of its twelve edges. (7:4; 14:1; textual note to 21:16—New Jerusalem is seen as a cubic city whose dimensions, in Greek, are twelve thousand stadia on a side by twelve edges on a cube = 144,000!)

● Present this information to your class members at the begining of this activity. Ask:

—What observations can you make? (This illustration can be used to discuss with the class the vision's revelation of the transition from the first covenant community of God's people to the final covenant community that emerges out of the first but also transcends it.)

(F) Shake the status quo.

● Prior to class time read the article "Shaking the Status Quo" (page 28) to supply you information for this learning option. Read the following information aloud to your class members as an introduction for this activity.

The first (6:12) and last (16:18) mentions of "earthquake" in the vision significantly contain the only two mentions of the islands and mountains being disturbed.

Islands and mountains were important points of reference for a culture whose topographical center was the Mediterranean Sea. Much of this culture's commerce moved across the Mediterranean. Therefore the disruption of navigational points of reference would result in disorientation.

In all the instances of earthquakes, disruptions of sun, moon, stars, mountains, and islands in the vision, the citizens of the rebellious order are still in existence.

● Divide your class members into four groups. Ask each small group to look up earthquake references.

Group One: 8:5
When the incandescent prayers of the saints are cast into the earth (the fallen order) there is an earthquake.

Group Two: 11:15-19
At the close of the seven trumpets, with the ascription of praise because God has begun to reign and the time for destroying the destroyers of the earth has come, there is again an earthquake. In both instances, the earthquake depicts the effect of the presence of God in the fallen order.

Group Three: 11:13
At the resurrection and ascension of the two witnesses there is a "great" earthquake and a tenth of the city falls and 7,000 humans are killed.

Group Four: 16:18-19
At the close of the seven bowls there is another "great" earthquake (16:18), an amplification of the "great" earthquake that shook the city where Jesus was crucified by noting that "the great city" was split into three parts and God remembered "great" Babylon to make her drain the cup of the fury of God's wrath (16:18-19).

● After the small groups have done their research, ask:

—What did the earthquake symbolize? (The presence of God and the working of God in the midst of the rebellious order)

—Can you think of other biblical references when the presence of God was symbolized in an earthquake?

—Remember that the Mediterranean area was subject to earthquakes quite often. What natural manifestation of God's presence would be most meaningful for your congregation?

Dimension 3:
What Does the Bible Mean to Us?

(G) Study the image of the altar.

● For this activity you will need a concordance.

● Share the following information with your class members:

The Greek term for *altar* has an interesting history. It first appears in the Greek translation of the Old Testament and, until the time of Codex Justinianeus, a body of civil law (A.D. 529–565), is found only in Jewish and Christian literature. It is always used for the altar of Yahweh in the

Greek Old Testament. Another term is employed for pagan altars. The altar of Yahweh was the place of cleansing, renewing, transforming encounter with God. It was the place where the sacrifices were offered through which the people of God affirmed their covenant relationship with God and were cleansed and renewed in that relationship. You might want to read from a concordance some of the different references to the word *altar* to see how it has been used in the Old Testament.

This understanding of sacrifice is more fully developed in the early church. Ignatius writes to the Philadelphians (around A.D. 100–110), "Be zealous, therefore, to use one Eucharist [Communion, Lord's Supper]; for there is one flesh of our Lord Jesus Christ and one cup for union with his blood, one altar, as there is one Bishop together with the elders and deacons my fellow servants, in order that whatever you do you might do according to God." The suggestion is that the Eucharist is the altar where God's people come into fullness of relationship with God.

● After hearing this historical background for *altar*, ask your class members to think about their own understanding of *altar*. Ask:
—Do you remember your childhood understanding of your church's altar?
—What is considered sacred in your church's sanctuary?
● Reflect on how different denominations convey the sense of the sacred in sanctuary structure.
—How is the concept of sacred conveyed today?
—When you participate in Communion (Eucharist), how is this a sacred time for you?
—What is your understanding of *sacrifice*? of *altar*?

(H) Is God's presence a disruptive presence?

● For this learning option you will need chalkboard and chalk or a large sheet of paper and markers.
● Share the following information as a way to begin:
The image of the release of the troubling, disruptive, disturbing presence of God in the midst of the world through the prayers of the saints brings us back to consideration of the fifth and sixth seals.
The sixth seal reveals that the Fallen Babylon world is not pleased with the presence of God in its midst. In fact, it is convulsed and its whole order of being is disoriented. It does everything in its power to evade and avoid God's presence in its midst. It even removes the causes of God's presence in its midst as seen in the fifth seal.
● Ask the class to develop a list of illustrations of how faithful discipleship releases God's disruptive presence in the fallen order. List these on your chalkboard.
● Brainstorm ways in which faithful Christian discipleship would be disruptive to those who maintain the status quo.
—What might be some of the consequences of faithfulness in that situation?

(I) Consider the profound power of prayer.

One of the most powerful images in John's vision is the seventh seal. It is a profound revelation of the nature of prayer.
● Have the class members review the basis for the imagery of the seventh seal from the study book (page 46). Divide your class members into three groups.
● Assign **Group One** to study and report on the Day of Atonement and what it meant in the Jewish tradition (Leviticus 16).
● Assign **Group Two** to study the relationship between prayer and incense in Judaism.
● Ask **Group Three** to report on the aspects of theophanies (manifestations of God's presence) in the Old Testament as they relate to thunder, rumblings, lightning, and earthquake.
● With the above information before them, lead the class members to discuss why the vision uses Day of Atonement imagery as the context for the prayers of the saints.
—What does this reveal about the costliness of true prayer?
—What kind of relationship with God is portrayed here as the context of prayer?
● Perhaps the most important aspect of the seventh seal's image of prayer is its outcome. More often than not the goal of prayer is to fulfill the needs, purposes, or desires of the one praying. Ask:
—What does John's vision of prayer as the release of God's presence into the world do to such a theology?

(J) Close with a hymn.

As you will have discussed in one of the above learning options, part of the power of the seventh seal is in the lives and prayers of the saints. An appropriate hymn to close this lesson would be "For All the Saints" (*The United Methodist Hymnal*, 711). If you have a pianist in your class, arrange ahead of time for accompaniment for this closing hymn. Have enough hymnals so that all can participate in the singing.

Additional Bible Helps

Who's That Man on the White Horse?
There has been much discussion over the identity of the first rider (6:2). The two basic positions are that the first rider is either Christ or a militaristic, antichrist figure. The basic arguments against the figure being Christ are based on (1) the difficulty of Christ being both the one who opens the seal and the one who rides forth; and (2) the rider having a bow, which represents militarism, whereas Christ on the white horse in 19:11-16 has a sword coming from his mouth, which is the word of God.

The arguments against the rider being Christ are weak. In

the dynamics of a vision there is no problem with Christ being both the one who opens the seal and the one who rides forth, especially since it is the death of Jesus that discloses the deep purposes of God; and his death is his conquering (5:5-6). It is the death of the Lamb that manifests forth the victory that has conquered the realm of rebellion.

The contrast between the bow and the sword may be overly drawn. The sword in the mouth of Christ in 19:15 and 21 is the instrument by which he "strikes the nations" and that by which the army of the beast and false prophet is slain. Thus, if the bow of the first rider is a weapon of conquest, it would simply be a modulation of the image and would not separate the first rider from Christ. But the bow may not be a weapon of conquest. In Genesis 9:13 and following, God gives the bow as a sign of the covenant between God and the creation using, in the Greek version, the same term used by John to describe the first rider's bow. The image of the bow, therefore, may represent God's covenant not to destroy the creation because of its rebellion, but to conquer the rebellion through the death of the Lamb.

The shift from a crown on the rider to diadems on Christ (19:12) is also misunderstood by those who see it as proof that the rider is not Christ. Only heavenly or redeemed figures have crowns in the vision. The one use of *crown* that seems to be the exception is the presence of crowns on the locusts of the fifth trumpet (9:7). But they have upon their heads something "as" crowns "like" gold, but not golden crowns. It would seem, therefore, that the first rider is a heavenly figure because he wears a golden crown.

The crown given to the first rider may be the crown of life, which has already been introduced in the letters to the churches (2:10; 3:11). This would enhance the image of the bow as a sign of God's covenant with creation. The covenant not to destroy creation because of its rebellion brings forth an alternative means of dealing with the rebellion, one that results in life and not destruction.

And Who's on the Red Horse?

The identification of this figure (6:3-4) is suggested by the color of the horse. In the entire New Testament the term *fiery* (NRSV: "red") appears only twice. The other appearance is in John's description of the dragon (12:3) that instigates warfare in heaven (12:7). (Chapter 7 will give a closer look at this dragon image.) The outcome of the warfare is the defeat of the dragon and its forces followed by the statement: "There was no longer any place for them in heaven" (12:8), and Satan is thrown down to the earth (12:9). The "peace" of God's realm has no place for those who would rebel against the sovereignty of God, which is the source of that peace. The rebellion itself breaks the peace. The rebels, by their own action, exclude themselves from the peace of God.

Since Satan was cast down into the earth, it would not be surprising to learn that he "takes the peace from the earth."

John is seeing the deeper dimensions that lie behind the activities of the second rider. This suggests that the second rider is Satan.

Shaking the Status Quo

Throughout the Old Testament and in the larger Roman world the earthquake was an image for the presence of God as well as a sign of the displeasure of the gods. In the Old Testament the presence of God in the midst of the enemies of God's people is characterized by earthquake.

Throughout John's vision the earthquake is a consistent image for the presence and action of God in the midst of the fallen order. It seems obvious from the development of the earthquake image in the vision that the earthquake, particularly the "great" earthquake, portrays the effect of the presence of God and the working of God's purposes in the midst of the rebellious order.

It must also be remembered that John was conveying his vision to people who lived in an active earthquake zone. Even today disastrous earthquakes continue to shake that part of the earth. It was an image that would not have been lost on John's readers. It was not merely a theoretical symbol—it was a dynamic reality of life.

Angels

There are three groups of seven angels: the angels of the seven churches, the angels with the seven trumpets, and the angels with the seven bowls. Perhaps all three groups are one and the same. As noted in the discussion of the angels/messengers of the churches, when the representatives of the synagogue congregation came to bring the prayers of the people before God, they stood before the ark of the Torah, the synagogue representation for the presence of God. In other words, they would "stand in the presence of God." It may be that the description of the seven angels as "standing before God" identifies them as the "messengers" of the seven churches who bring the prayers of the saints to God.

When John says that he saw "the" seven angels, rather than simply "seven angels," he suggests either some specific antecedent (like the angels of the seven churches) or a specific group of angels known to his readers. In the Jewish tradition out of which the early church emerged, there were seven "angels of the Presence" who stood in the presence of God. This image goes back at least to Isaiah (63:9) and is found often in Jubilees. Even if the vision is not portraying the messengers of the seven churches but the angels of the Presence, their association with the prayers of the saints retains the connection between the "angels" of the seven churches, those who represent the people of God in prayer, and the seven angels with the seven trumpets. This is especially the case since the action of the seventh seal, from which the angels with the trumpets emerge, focuses upon the "prayers of the saints."

6

Revelation 8:6–11:19

TRUMPETS OF DOOM AND DELIGHT

LEARNING MENU

Choose at least one activity from each Dimension, keeping in mind the learning methods that seem to work best with your class members.

Dimension 1:
What Does the Bible Say?

(A) Work with the study book questions.

1. The similarities in comparing the first four trumpets and the first four bowls are the location of the action of the trumpets and bowls—earth, sea, rivers and springs, sun. On one hand, these elements are the basic essentials of life on this planet. On the other hand, earth and sea are also used as images of the rebellious order throughout John's vision, and, in the case of the bowls, the action is against those who have the mark of the beast.

It should be noted that an important distinction is made after the fourth trumpet. The rest of the trumpets are directed toward "the inhabitants of the earth" (8:13), the vision's designation for the citizens of Fallen Babylon.

2. The angel in 10:1 is Jesus. The attributes of the angel in 10:1-2a make it almost certain that it is Jesus. The mingling of attributes of Jesus at the beginning of the vision (wrapped in a cloud; face like the sun; legs like pillars of fire; voice like a lion) and the attributes of God in Revelation 4 (rainbow over his head; voice like thunders; scroll in his hand) suggest that this is a vision of God in Christ involved with the fallen order.

Additional Discussion: In order to gather additional background information about the identity of the angel in 10:1, your class might want to divide into two groups and do the following activity.

Group One can make a list of the attributes of all the individual angelic beings in Revelation, looking especially at the angelic figures in 7:2; 8:3-5, 10; 18:1, 21; 20:1-3; and 22:6, 16. These attributes should then be compared with those of God and the Lamb in John's vision.

Group Two can study the angelic appearances of God in the Old Testament, looking especially at Genesis 16:7-12; 21:17-19; 31:11-13; Exodus 3:2-12; Judges 6:11-24; 13:8-23. One outcome should be to note how the angel and God seem to merge in these accounts. The angel is God; God is the angel.

This activity should help in understanding what John says in Revelation 1:1 when the one who appears to him is Jesus and in understanding what Jesus says in 22:16 about sending his angel.

3. The two witnesses are symbols for Moses and Elijah who, in turn, represent the law and the prophets—the structure of the old covenant community.

It is also significant to note that the time of their activity concludes with their participation in the crucifixion, resurrection, and ascension of Jesus.

Additional Discussion: The class might want to discuss this in light of Jesus' statement, "Do not think I have come to abolish the law or the prophets; I have come not to abolish but to fulfill" (Matthew 5:17). In what way did Jesus "fulfill" the law and the prophets? How does that fulfillment relate to his crucifixion?

Dimension 2:
What Does the Bible Mean?

(B) How long did you say?

- Prior to class time read the artitle in the Additional Bible Helps, "Forty-two Months—1,260 Days—Time, Times, Half-a-Time." This section has information you will want to include in your discussion.
- Ask your class members to list the time references in 11:2; 11:3; 12:6; 12:14; and 13:5. Then ask:
—What connection is there among them?
- Tell the class that the significant factor here is that the 42-month, 1,260-day, 3½ year period represents a time of pressure upon the faithful by those who rebel against God.

If there are concerns by any in the class about whether these time references are literal, discuss the symbolic use of time references. In a vision so filled with images and symbols, the first presumption about the time images should be that they, too, are pointers to a deeper reality and not literal indicators of time.

This may be part of what John is signaling to us when he uses three different means to describe the same period of time (42 months, 1,260 days, 3½ years = a time, and times, and half-a-time). It should be noted that this period of time always relates to people associated with New Jerusalem in their relationship with Fallen Babylon and, particularly, their oppression or death at the hands of Fallen Babylon and its agents.

(C) Explore the idea of a depleted creation.

Advance Preparation

If there is a scientist in the class, or if one is available in the church, have her or him describe to the class the principle of entropy, which operates in the physical universe. If this is not possible, perhaps one of the members of the class could research the topic in advance of the session and report the findings during the session. (In a nutshell, this principle holds that the universe is running down.)

- With the principle of entropy as a framework, ask the class to discuss what John is seeing in the first four trumpets. (One of the outcomes should be the understanding that at least part of what John is seeing is a created order that is flawed and not fully supportive of human wholeness and well-being.)
- Then ask the class to think together about why the last three trumpets are designated as focused upon the participants in the rebellious order ("the inhabitants of the earth"—8:13, and "those people who do not have the seal of God on their foreheads"—9:4).
- Ask:
—Can we infer from these references that the effects of the first four trumpets are upon all humanity, both God's people and those who rebel against God?
—Is John seeing the nature of the natural order within which all human existence is lived?
- Remind the class that Paul speaks of creation's "bondage to decay" (Romans 8:21). This seems to express the same idea.

(D) Study the torment of sin.

- For this learning option you need a concordance, paper, pens or pencils.
- Divide the class into two groups.
- Ask **Group One** in the class to research the nature of locusts and their activity. This group might also look at the way in which locusts are portrayed in the Scriptures.
- Ask **Group Two** to research the nature of scorpions and the effects of their sting on humans. This group, too, might study the role of scorpions in the Scriptures.
- With the input from these two groups, have the entire class discuss the implications of the vision's imagery. It seems to have something to do with an inexorable reality that is extremely painful and debilitating.
- The group should also discuss the image of wanting to die but not being able to do so.
- Ask:
—Why isn't suicide an option?
—Is physical death what the vision is portraying?
—Could this be a desire to die to that which is causing the torment?
NOTE: All of the above issues must be seen in the context

of the nature of the one whom the vision portrays as "king" over the hoards of locust-scorpions. He is "The Destroyer."

(E) Illustrate and discuss the destructiveness of sin.

Another aspect of the infinite number of the cavalry is the inexorable reality of the consequences of rebellion against God. As shall be seen later in the seven bowls, this is not an image of a vengeful, wrathful, punitive, vindictive deity. It is simply the nature of the reality of rebellion. As Paul puts it, "The wages of sin is death" (Romans 6:23). The image of this hoard being prepared for the hour, day, month, and year also reveals that this is not a reactionary response to rebellion. It is one that has been in place all along.

- If there are any artists in the class, ask them to draw for the group their renditions of the appearance of the horses and riders. Have paper, crayons, markers, and/or pencils available for this activity.
- Then ask the group to discuss a number of features of the horses and riders.
—Is there any relationship between the horses' heads being like lions' heads (9:17) and Jesus being portrayed as the Lion of Judah (5:5)?
—Why is there such a close correlation between the breastplates of the riders and what comes forth from the horses' mouths (fire, smoke, sulfur)?
—Is there any connection with the fire and sulfur and smoke mentioned again in 14:10-11 and the lake of fire and sulfur in 19:20; 20:10; and 21:8?
NOTE: It is of crucial importance for the class to note that the focus of the action in the sixth seal (as in the seven bowls in chapter 16) is not destruction but repentance (9:20-21)! While destruction is the inevitable consequence of rebellion, it is not the only option available. The group might want to discuss why those who see the destructiveness of sin in the lives of others do not turn away from it themselves.

(F) Study the sovereign angelic Christ.

The interludes in the series of sevens are interesting. The six seals revealed God's conquering rider and the destructive riders of the rebellion as the operative realities of human history. These realities result in the martyrdom of faithful citizens of New Jerusalem at the hands of Fallen Babylon and the disorienting disruption of Fallen Babylon by God's presence in its midst. John then sees the "roll call" of the redeemed and their joyous worship of God around the throne.

(Preview of upcoming events: After the six bowls that depict the torment of Fallen Babylon caused by God's holiness in its midst and its preparation for war with God—that would mean an intensification of its persecution of God's people—John hears, in a mini-interlude, the promise of Christ's coming and the third of the seven blessings [16:15] to those who remain faithful in the midst of such conditions.)

And here, after six trumpets that have disclosed the radically flawed condition of the natural order and the destructive character of the rebellious order, a picture of dark despair, John sees an interlude of Christ standing in sovereignty over the rebellious order with his feet on the sea and the earth—the two primary images for the rebellious order. The triple repetition of this posture suggests perfect (the image of three) or absolute sovereignty.

- Explore the number of puzzles in this portion of the vision. Discuss the following ideas and questions with your class members:
—What are the seven thunders? (The class might study the image of thunder in the Old Testament, especially Exodus 19:16-19, where thunder and trumpets are combined.)
—What is the little scroll in Christ's hand, and why is it open rather than sealed? (The class might study Ezekiel 2:9–3:3 as the source of John's image.)
—What is the mystery to be revealed in the seventh trumpet? (Have the group study Revelation 11:15-19, the seventh trumpet, and discuss what is revealed there that fulfills what God had given to the prophets.)
—Who are "they" who speak to John in 10:11?

(G) Study God's redeeming victory.

Revelation 11:3-13 is one of the crucial foci of John's vision. Here John sees the profound dimensions of what took place upon the cross of Christ. The old covenant was consummated, God's victory over the death of Fallen Babylon was manifested, the ultimate demise of the rebellious order was affirmed, and redemption was made possible for the citizens of Fallen Babylon.

- Ask a class member to read aloud Revelation 11:3-13.
- Ask students to read in their study books, if they have not already done so, the section on the two witnesses, page 55.
- Ask a class member to read aloud the Gospel account of the Transfiguration (Matthew 17:1-8; Mark 9:2-8; or Luke 9:28-36).
- Then discuss the following questions with your class members:
—Who are these two witnessess?
—What parts of the old covenant do they represent?
—What is their role here in Revelation?
—What parts of this section of the vision surprise you or concern you?

Dimension 3: What Does the Bible Mean to Us?

(H) Develop evidences of a flawed creation.

- Brainstorm with the class to develop evidences of the flawed character of the created order.

- Ask:
—Is there any connection between the fallen condition of human existence and the burgeoning environmental crises that face us in our day? Why or why not?
—Can our spirituality be separated from our createdness and our participation in the created order? Why or why not?
—Do you see a relationship between all our environmental crises and manifestations of the prevailing spirituality of our culture? How?
—Which spirituality is more closely related to the current state of our environment, Fallen Babylon or New Jerusalem?
- Have the class develop a "manifesto" (declaration of intent) of the environmental impact of New Jerusalem spirituality.

(I) Illustrate the torment and destructiveness of sin.

- Bring a copy of a current Sunday or daily newspaper to today's session. Also you will need paper, scissors, glue, tape, and markers for this learning option.
- Give each individual or groups of individuals a section of the newspaper and ask them to cut out examples of the torment of sin or the destructiveness of sin.
- Instruct your class members to make these newspaper selections into a collage to illustrate the fifth and sixth trumpets and hang in the class space as a reminder of one of the realities God is responding to redemptively in John's vision.
- There may be some in the class who can give an illustration of how, when people see the destructiveness of sin in the lives of others, they continue in the same activities—a contemporary illustration of Revelation 9:20-21.

(J) Give personal experiences of redeeming grace.

- Some people do not feel comfortable talking of their personal experiences of God in a large group. Be sensitive to this feeling and divide your class into small groups if doing so seems that it might encourage participation.
- Ask if anyone in the group would be willing to share with the class their experience of transferring their citizenship from Fallen Babylon to New Jerusalem, living illustrations of Revelation 11:13b—those who came to stand in awe of God and give God glory.
- Talk together as a class about "citizenship" in New Jerusalem or Fallen Babylon. What traits of the New Jerusalem do you hold? your congregation? Encourage individuals to probe her or his own heart to see whether the values and perspectives of New Jerusalem or Fallen Babylon are prevalent.
- This time of reflection lends itself for people to talk about their experiences of God in their lives and how that experience of God changed (or did not change) them.

- If this is your closing class activity, you may want to conclude this reflection time with your class by singing "Amazing Grace" (*The United Methodist Hymnal*, 378).

REMINDER: Be sensitive to new people in your class who may not have been involved in the church very long. Even a hymn as familiar as "Amazing Grace" is not known to everyone.

(K) Study the image of a "trampled temple."

- Ask a class member to read aloud Revelation 11:1-2.
- Then discuss how in our community of faith, your congregation is being "trampled" by the Fallen Babylon world in which we live (Revelation 11:1-2).
- Ask the following:
—What are some of the crucial issues of the community in which the class's congregation exists?
—What should the congregation be and/or do in this situation to be faithful citizens of New Jerusalem?
—In what way might the congregation experience "trampling" if it were faithful?
—How is your congregation called to be Christ's servant in the world?
—What risks are involved?
- If this is your closing activity, close by singing the hymn, "When the Church of Jesus" (*The United Methodist Hymnal*, 592). Ask an instrumentalist ahead of time to be prepared to accompany the class. As an alternative to singing this hymn, ask three persons to each read aloud a stanza.

Additional Bible Helps

Some Important Elements in John's Vision

Midheaven. "Midheaven" throughout the vision seems to be a place associated with the condition of the fallen order. In 14:6 and the following verses, a series of three angels appear in "midheaven." The first proclaims the gospel to "those who live on the earth," to "every nation and tribe and language and people" (14:6), thus evangelizing the citizens of Fallen Babylon. The second proclaims the fallen nature of Babylon (14:8), and the third gives a warning about the ultimate destiny of those who worship the beast and its image and receive its mark (14:9-11).

In 19:17, John sees an angel call to the birds of prey that fly in "midheaven" to gather to eat the slain army of the beast (19:17, 21).

The fact that the three "woes" in 8:13 are for "the inhabitants of the earth" (the consistent image for the citizens of the rebellious order) is consistent with the image of "midheaven" being related to the condition of Fallen Babylon.

Falling Stars. The fallen star of the vision is obviously a heavenly being. This is also a consistent image in the vision. Jesus himself is the bright morning star (22:16), and the third of the stars of heaven that the dragon sweeps down with his tail represent those heavenly beings who joined him in his rebellion (12:4). The image of heavenly beings or angels as stars was common in the pool of imagery available to John and his readers.

There is an interesting parallel to this portion of the vision in Luke's Gospel. Jesus tells his disciples, "I watched Satan *fall from heaven* like a flash of lightning. See, I have given you authority to tread on *snakes and scorpions*, and over all the power of the enemy; and nothing will hurt you" (Luke 10:18-19; italics added). In the fifth trumpet, the star that had *fallen from heaven* releases locusts that have the authority of *scorpions* (Revelation 9:3, 5, 10), and in the sixth trumpet the power of the horses is in their tails, which are like *serpents* (9:19). Since the fifth and sixth trumpets exempt those who have the seal of God upon their foreheads (9:4, 20 and following.), it appears that John's vision portrays the same reality as Jesus' statement.

The Abyss. The *abyss* (author's translation; "pit" or "bottomless pit," NRSV) in both Hellenistic and Jewish cultures was used to denote both the primitive ocean or floods of water and the realm of the dead. In later Judaism it came to be understood as the place of rebellious beings (see Jude 6; 2 Peter 2:4).

With these antecedents for the term, it is most probable that in John's vision, *abyss* is another term for Death and Hades or for the sea as the realm of rebellion. This is substantiated later in the vision when the beast ascends from the abyss (11:7; 17:8) and appears to be the same beast that ascends from the sea in 13:1. The abyss as the place of rebellious beings is certainly present when Jesus casts Satan into the abyss (20:3), and Jesus' possession of the keys of Death and of Hades (1:18) seems to be paralleled by his possession of the key of the abyss in 20:1.

The Little Scroll. The antecedent for John's experience is found in Ezekiel. Ezekiel was given a little scroll by God, which was associated with what God said: "Hear what I say to you . . . open your mouth and eat what I give you" (Ezekiel 2:8). Ezekiel was to absorb God's word into his own being and then manifest it forth in his witness. When Ezekiel ate the scroll, it was as sweet as honey in his mouth (Ezekiel 3:3). Jeremiah also speaks of finding God's words and eating them (Jeremiah 15:16). For Jeremiah, also, this

experience is at the heart of his prophesying. The image is one of completely absorbing the words of God so that they become the operative principle of one's life. John seems to have so absorbed the scroll of the old covenant that he is able to proclaim its profound fulfillment in Christ in Revelation 11:1-13.

Like Ezekiel and Jeremiah, the scroll is sweet in John's mouth. This seems to be the experience of the psalmist:

"How sweet are your words to my taste,
      sweeter than honey to my mouth" (Psalm 119:103).

"More to be desired are they than gold,
      even much fine gold;
sweeter also than honey
      and drippings of the honeycomb" (Psalm 19:10).

But for John, the scroll becomes bitter in his stomach. There seem to be no antecedents for this image. John's prophecy following the eating of the scroll (11:1-13) reveals the sweetness of God's victory in Christ through the bitterness of the Crucifixion. John seems to experience the sweetness of New Jerusalem and the bitterness of Fallen Babylon.

Forty-two Months—1,260 Days—Time, Times, Half-a-Time. The forty-two month, 1,260-day period has a history in the life of God's covenant people. In the days of Elijah when Israel was led astray into the worship of Baal by Jezebel, Elijah prayed; and there was a drought for forty-two months (1 Kings 16:29–18:46).

At the time of the Babylonian captivity, the Babylonian response to Zedekiah's revolt covered a period of about forty-two months (Jeremiah 52).

In the Maccabean revolt against Antiochus Epiphanes, the period of desolation from the desecration of the Temple by Antiochus until its cleansing and restoration under Judas was about three years.

If John's vision came after the destruction of Jerusalem in A.D. 70, the Roman siege of Jerusalem lasted from March of A.D. 67 until September of A.D. 70, exactly forty-two months.

In each of these instances, the people of God experienced severe tribulation, either at the hand of God for their unfaithfulness or at the hand of their enemies. It would seem, therefore, that the image of forty-two months in John's vision indicates a period of tribulation for God's faithful people. But it should not be taken as a literal forty-two months. It is, rather, another image for the tribulation that New Jerusalem experiences at the hands of Fallen Babylon.

7

Revelation 12:1-17

GOD THE MOTHER

Dimension 1:
What Does the Bible Say?

(A) Answer the questions in the study book.

1. God as a woman.

TEACHING TIP
Discussion of the idea that God appears in John's vision in chapter 12 as a woman may be more than sufficient to occupy the entire class time. Given the present climate in the church with regard to feminine images for God, and the powerful emotions engaged when the issue arises, it may be difficult for the class to wrestle with a biblical image of God as a woman, and a pregnant woman at that. Perhaps the class might agree together to set aside differences of opinion and perspective for the sake of the study of this portion of Revelation and let the text and its imagery become the focus of attention.

Invite those who have difficulty with this feminine image of God to recognize that God is referred to in many ways, that no one image can convey the total nature of God. This question is a subjective one. Entertain the positive and negative thoughts on this God as a woman/mother image.

If your class wants to continue discussion on this image, a good follow-up learning activity would be activity (C).

2. A discussion of the dragon's attempt to devour the woman's child should be geared to help the class realize the essential nature of rebellion against God. Rebellion is not simply a matter of going our own way. *Rebellion is a matter of taking the role of God for ourselves.* In this context, the class might reflect upon Genesis 3:5 where the original temptation was to "be like God."

Additional Discussion: It might also be helpful for some discussion to focus on the attempt to bring God under control, another aspect of the vision of "devouring" the woman's child. If the dragon can take the essence of God into its own being, then it has encompassed God within itself, thus bringing God under its control.

3. Many interesting aspects of the war in heaven might be raised by the participant's responses to this question. One that should receive special attention is the revelation that even in heaven there is freedom to rebel against God. Often the idea is held that heaven is a place of eternal security where there will never be any temptation to trouble our lives and, of course, no thought of rebellion against God. The

vision seems to be showing us that God has created beings for a relationship with God that is freely entered into or just as freely rejected. It seems that if our yes to the relationship is to have any meaning and validity, then we must be equally free to say no to the relationship.

4. You Mean It's Over Already?

TEACHING TIP

Ask the class where the "Hallelujah Chorus" comes in Handel's *Messiah*. It might be a good idea to look at a score of *Messiah* or even bring one to class. Many people think the "Hallelujah Chorus" is the finale of the oratorio and are surprised to discover that it comes only slightly over halfway into the work.

It would seem that Handel grasped the same reality that John sees at this point in his vision (12:10). For the vision, however, the victory song is, for all practical purposes, the opening aria! John seems to be seeing that God's victory over the dragon's rebellion comes not at the end of a long, protracted warfare but is already present in the very nature of God before the rebellion.

Dimension 2: What Does the Bible Mean?

(B) Explore signs and portents.

TEACHING TIP

The use of *like* and *as* with other images reveal John's struggle to convey in language an experience that transcends language. Note that images depict rather than describe; they are fluid, not fixed. All this suggests that the vision reality is much too complex to be contained by frail human language.

Note the occasions when John uses *like* and *as* in Revelation. They are usually used with reference to the images, symbols, and sounds within the vision.

- Ask the class to clarify its understanding that John is signaling his readers that even the imagery he uses to convey his visionary experience is incapable of conveying the fullness of what he experienced.
- For this learning option you will need concordances, paper, pens or pencils.
- Divide the class members into four small groups. Divide the Book of Revelation by chapters and assign each group several chapters to look up the use of *like* and *as*. A concordance will make finding these references easy.

  NOTE: These particular references are sometimes located in an appendix rather than the main section.
- After the groups have about ten minutes to check their

findings, ask a group representative to tell the whole class of the references within the chapters they researched.
- Then ask the class to discuss how John signaled the readers of more profound aspects of a visionary experience.
- The outcome of this exercise should be the realization that at this point John's vision is moving into the most profound realities of the entire vision. He struggles with words to convey the meaning of what he experienced in his vision.

(C) Explore the God/Mother image.

If your class members desire follow-up research and discussion on the Mother/God image, this learning option should help facilitate discussion.

Advance Preparation

Prior to class time photocopy the article in the Additional Bible Helps "Who Is That Woman?" for class distribution in Part Two.

Part One:
- For Part One of this learning option have several concordances, Bible dictionary, various Bible translations, paper, pens or pencils available for this session. (Two concordances based on the NRSV include *The NRSV Concordance*, by John R. Kohlenberger, Zondervan, 1991, and *NRSV Exhaustive Concordance*, by Bruce M. Metzger, Nelson, 1991. Others are available for the various Bible translations.) Divide your class members into four groups. Assign the groups the following research:
- Ask **Group One** to research Old Testament images of fire, light, brightness, and sun associated with God. (If you do not have access to a concordance, here are a few examples: *fire*—Exodus 3:2 ; 19:18; Numbers 11:1; Deuteronomy 4:24; Isaiah 66:15; *light*—Job 29:3; 33:30; Psalm 4:6; 27:1; 119:105; Isaiah 2:5; 9:2; 49:6; *brightness*—Isaiah 59:9; Habakkuk 3:4; *sun*—Psalm 84:11; Malachi 4:2.)
- Ask **Group Two** to research Old Testament images of stars and crown for the twelve tribes of Israel. (A few examples: *stars*—Genesis 22:17; 26:4; Deuteronomy 1:10; 1 Chronicles 27:23; *crown*—Isaiah 62:3; Zechariah 9:16.)
- Ask **Group Three** to research Old Testament images that involve the moon, especially in connection with worship, sabbath, and festivals. (The use of a Bible dictionary will work best here.)
- Ask **Group Four** to research Old Testament images of eagles's wings associated with God as well as other images of wings associated with God. (A few examples: Deuteronomy 32:10-11; Exodus 19:4; Psalm 17:8; 36:7; 57:1; 63:7; 91:4.)
- After the small groups have had ten minutes to do their research, ask a person from each group to report. Then

discuss the attributes of the woman in John's vision (Revelation 12:1, 14).

● Ask:

—What do the findings tell of the similarities and differences between the woman and God?

Part Two:

If additional discussion is desired, distribute copies of the article, "Who Is That Woman?" from Additional Bible Helps to your class members. Allow a few minutes for them to read over the article. Ask for responses and insights from the article.

● This Mother/God image is very powerful and complex. As addressed in the article, throughout the ages of study and reflection on Revelation, this woman image has also been thought to be Wisdom, Israel, the New Jersalem, Mary (mother of Jesus).

● Read aloud from the study book, page 63, "A Pre-existent Incarnation."

● Note that this is what Paul sensed when, after noting the deep, painful groanings of creation for redemption (Romans 8:22), and the deep, painful groanings of the redeemed for the fulfillment of their redemption (8:23), he stated that the Spirit itself has deep, painful groanings for the consummation of redemption (8:26).

TEACHING TIP

While studying this complex passage, many questions may arise. One question relating to verses 5 and 6 of the chapter concerns how the Woman/God can birth a son; have the child snatched from the dragon and taken to God's throne; then flee into the wilderness where God has prepared a place for her. How can God be in two places at one time?

Remember that this is a vision. Visions do not have to follow a human sequential ordering. (Like in 6:2 the basic arguments against the figure being Christ are based on the difficulty of Christ being both the one who opens the seal and the one who rides forth.) However, it is the death of Jesus that discloses the deep purposes of God; and his death is his conquering (5:5-6). It is the death of the Lamb that manifests forth the victory that has conquered the realm of rebellion. Christ's death and thus the conquering of the realm of the rebellion, is the focus, not *how* Christ could be in two places at once. In a vision (like in our own dreams) amazing things can happen.

Another important element of this event in the son's birth, the snatching from the dragon, and the deliverence to the throne is that only God is worthy to act on God's behalf.

Try to guide your class members to see the larger picture of God's great love for creation, a love so great that God would bring forth a child into the face of the rebellious one in order to redeem the creation.

● Note also how the richness of this image comes alive as we see God's great love poured out for the redemption of a rebellious creation even before it rebelled.

(D) Probe the depths of God's redeeming love.

● Divide your class members into three groups and have them spend a few minutes reading and discussing the following Old Testament passages that describe God's love for the people of God:

Group One—Isaiah 49:14-16
Group Two— Hosea 2:14–3:1
Group Three— Hosea 11:1-9

● Have the class then discuss John's vision in the context of the Old Testament images, particularly:

—the profound depths of God's love for God's rebellious people manifested in the Old Testament images and how that idea is magnified in John's vision;

—the fact that God's profound love is not something God "developed" after the rebellion but is the essence of the very being of God even before Satan rebelled.

● Ask:

—How do these Old Testament images of God's love for Israel support or discredit the image of God's love given in chapter 12 of Revelation?

● Probe together as a class the image of God bringing forth God's very being into the mouth of the dragon. (God's response to the rebellion is not an "arms length" managerial or administrative response. Neither is it a counter power play to that of the rebel, overcoming force with force. It is the victory of the infinite integrity and wholeness of God's being over evil's strongest move.)

(E) Study desert doings.

Part One:

● For this learning option you will need several large sheets of paper to tape on the wall for making a mural (about three feet by five feet), tape, old magazines (especially magazines that show desert scenes), crayons, glue, and markers.

● Invite class members to make a contribution to the desert mural. Contributions will vary from gluing a magazine picture to drawing a rock or other representative desert formation or creature.

Part Two:

● Then divide your class members into small groups. Ask the groups to look up Old Testament references to the desert and the wilderness, focusing on those passages that deal with the desert as a place where God works with God's people or as the place of evil spirits. (If your small groups have difficulty getting started, here are some examples: Exodus 19:2; Numbers 20:1; Deuteronomy 32:10; Psalm 106:13-15; Jeremiah 50:12.)

- Be prepared to share with the class the material in Additional Bible Helps, "The Desert in Jewish Perspective."
- Now look at the accounts of Jesus' temptation (Matthew 4:1-11 and its parallels in Mark 1:2-8 and Luke 3:1-20), as well as Matthew 24:24-26 and Acts 21:38, to develop some understanding of the perspective of the desert in first century Judaism.
- Ask the class then to analyze the role of the desert in John's vision as the location where the Woman/God has a "place" as well as the location of the dragon's warfare with the Woman/God. The desert was generally viewed as a lifeless place of destruction—an apt image for the realm of the "Destroyer" (Revelation 9:11). It is also a most suitable place for God's response to the rebellion, since God is the one who brings life out of death.

(F) Study the importance of *place*.

- Distribute to the class members these verses from Revelation that have the same Greek word for *place*: 2:5; 6:14; 12:6, 8, 14; 16:16; and 20:11.
- Have each person or group share how *place* is used in the assigned passage. Have them note especially how the use of *place* in their passage relates to relationship with God. (It appears that God is the definer of "place" [12:6, 14] and everything else has its "place" determined by its relationship with God.)

NOTE: The aim of this exercise is to realize that *place* is an image for a state of stability and integrity in relationship with God. If the Ephesian church doesn't return to its faithful, loving relationship with God, its lampstand (its very existence, since the "lampstand" is the church!) will be removed from its place (2:5). The fallen realm ("earth") and its encompassing environment ("sky") have no place apart from the presence of God (20:11). God's presence disrupts the "place" of Fallen Babylon's structures (mountains and islands—6:14). It seems that the only "place" Fallen Babylon has is a place of encounter with God (16:16), that is, it is conditioned by God's "place" not one of its own. This is revealed in the fact that there is no place for the dragon and its angels (12:8).

- Encourage class members's ideas and insights.

Dimension 3:
What Does the Bible Mean to Us?

(G) Who is in control in our relationship to God?

- Share the following thoughts on the issue of control with the class:

    Control is one of the focal issues of spiritual formation. The health of our spiritual lives is directly related to how much we try to control our relationship with God and how much God is in control. In fact, the deepest issue in every situation of our lives is whether we will allow God to be God in our lives or whether we will try to be God.

    In John's vision the dragon's attempt to "devour" God reveals to us the origin of our own tendency to want to keep God under our control.

- It is probably unlikely that there is anyone in the class who doesn't desire to be in relationship with God. Ask the class to investigate the nature of that relationship.
- Have each member of the class make a chart with nine squares in three rows of three. In the left-hand square of the top horizontal row have persons write in their three favorite activities with family or friends. In the left-hand box of the second horizontal row have persons list the three favorite aspects of their vocation. In the left-hand box of the bottom horizontal row, ask persons to list their three most desirable personal activities, activities they enjoy doing alone. (See the sample chart below.)
- In the second box of each vertical row, have students write in how much their relationship with God shapes each activity or behavior in the first box. Persons can use a scale of one to ten, or percentages, or simply such responses as "not at all," "a little," and so forth up to "completely."
- Then, in the third box of each vertical row, have persons indicate who is really in control of whatever level of relationship with God is indicated in the second boxes.

picnics	5	I am
camping	7	I am
movies	3	I am
organizing	4	I am
making speeches	3	I am
being outdoors	5	I am
listening to music	6	I am
reading	5	I am
taking walks	6	I am

- This exercise will help the participants begin to wrestle with the nature of their relationship with God and how much they retain control of the relationship even in those activities where they actively seek to operate out of a relationship with God. Help students to realize that most of us are perfectly willing to be in relationship with God as long as we can retain control of the relationship.

(H) Explore eternal security.

- Engage the class in discussion on another angle of the issue of control. The following material will provide you with a frame of reference by which the class could process the results of the previous exercise.
- Prepare to give a review on the following information to your class members:

The idea of a "war in heaven" has some profound implications for our understanding of relationship with God. John's vision of the war reveals that beings created by God for eternal relationship with God chose not to remain in that relationship. This suggests that relationship with God is not something that, once "achieved," can never be lost. Jesus seems to indicate this reality to the churches when he warns the church in Ephesus that unless it repents and returns to its first love he will remove their lampstand from its place (2:5). An even stronger warning is given to the church in Laodicea, which is in danger of being "spit" out of Jesus' mouth (3:15). Jesus tells the "dead" church in Sardis that it is possible to have one's name removed from the book of life (3:5).

In John's vision, the war in heaven is the direct consequence of the dragon's attempt to control God. This puts the results of the previous exercise in a new light. People who think they have their relationship with God all secure for eternity may be as far from reality as was the Laodicean church that believed it really had it all together, thinking "I am rich, I have prospered, and I need nothing," when, in reality, they were "wretched, pitiable, poor, blind, and naked" (3:17).

• Then ask your class members:
—Does the vision give us any perspective on what a genuine relationship with God is like?
• Ask a class member to read aloud Revelation 4:9-11. Then lead the class in a review of the following information:

As we saw in the fourth session, the image of the elders casting their crowns before the throne is an image of the relinquishment to God of control on one's relationship with God. It is the deep inner posture of desiring God to be God in one's life *on God's terms*. But, as the continual casting of the crowns by the elders reveals, this action can be reversed at any time. We are never robots in our relationship with God but persons who either freely and willingly allow God to be God on God's terms or take the control of our relationship with God into our own hands. When we take the control into our own hands, we begin to move into the shadow of the dragon and the danger of there being no place for us in heaven (12:7-8).

(I) We're all in our places.

If the class engaged in activity (F) in Dimension 2 on the use of *place*, they might want to carry this idea through to its implications for Christian discipleship.
• Have each member of the class list his or her center of identity, meaning, value, and purpose. For our culture in general, there are three basic centers from which individuals derive their identity, meaning, value, and purpose:
—what we do
—what we have
—what others think of us
For all too many people, even Christian disciples, one or

more of these centers construct the "place" of one's living.
• Ask the class to evaluate the centers they identified from a Christian perspective with relationship to these three basic options of our culture.
—Do they differ? If so, how?
(John's vision reveals that there is only one "place" of wholeness and integrity, one "place" where we find our true meaning, identity, value, and purpose. That place is in vital relationship with God. As John sees it, when relationship with God is flawed, there is "no place" for those persons in God's realm of wholeness and life.)

(J) How do we live a Christian life in the world?

• Ask class members to form conversation clusters. Then ask them to share with one another their understanding about Satan and the demonic realm. Ask:
—What does the dragon's war against the "rest" of the woman's children tell us about Christian life in the world?
• Ask a class member to read aloud Revelation 12:17.
• Introduce the following information to the class as a whole:
In our materialistic culture, we don't think much about Paul's assertion, "Our struggle is not against enemies of blood and flesh, but against the rulers, against the authorities, against the cosmic powers of this present darkness, against the spiritual forces of evil in the heavenly places" (Ephesians 6:12).
John's vision of the dragon warring against the children of the woman, "those who keep the commandments of God and hold the testimony of Jesus" (Revelation 12:17), indicates that human life is lived neither in a spiritual vacuum nor in a benign spiritual atmosphere.
• Then give the conversation groups ten minutes to discuss the following question:
—When a person begins a journey toward spiritual wholeness, what are the forces that work to lure them away from being in full relationship with God?
• Then ask another class member to read Revelation 12:11.
• Offer the following observation:
Here the vision moves to the historical dynamics of the life of citizens of New Jerusalem in the midst of Fallen Babylon. The victory of God's people over the dragon has three elements.
First, they conquer through the blood of the Lamb. How? By becoming partakers in the death of the Lamb. This points to the **second** element. "The word of their testimony" is living a life shaped by the image of Christ in a world shaped by the dragon. When this takes place, God's people may well find the death of Christ incarnate in their lives.
But this is the **third** element, "they did not cling to life even in the face of death." Even when the authority of the dragon is extended to its limits in slaying God's people, they continue to manifest the "word of their testimony,"

which conquers the dragon as they become joined in the death of Christ.

- Ask:
—How are we called as members of Christ's church to be servants in the world?
—How shall we praise God?
- Close this discussion by singing "See the Morning Sun Ascending" (*The United Methodist Hymnal*, 674). If this is an unfamiliar hymn, ask someone ahead of time to be prepared either to accompany on an instrument or lead the singing of the hymn. If singing is not an option, ask four people to each read a stanza.

Additional Bible Helps

Who Is That Woman?
The Woman has been identified as the following:
Wisdom (Proverbs 8, especially 22-31);
Israel (Hosea 2:19-20; Isaiah 62:5; Ezekiel 16:8-14;
    Jeremiah 2:2—these images are of Israel as the bride of
    Yahweh);
Heavenly Jerusalem (Galatians 4:26);
The church (Ephesians 5:25-27);
Mary, Jesus' mother.

Some have suggested that John's image derives from pagan combat myths, especially the myth of the pursuit of Leto (the mother of Apollo) by Python or the pursuit of Isis (the mother of Horus) by the red dragon Set-Typhon. Writing of the attributes of the Woman in Revelation 12, Collins says, "Such language is the ultimate in exaltation. Only a few goddesses of the Hellenistic and early Roman periods were awarded such honors." (*The Combat Myth in the Book of Revelation*, by Adela Y. Collins, Scholars Press, 1976) She then suggests Artemis and Isis as leading examples. Both goddesses lack full parallels to John's vision, however. Isis is the moon goddess associated with the sun, but without clear relationship to the zodiac. Artemis has zodiacal attributes and is usually pictured with the moon, but has no reference to the sun.

The attributes of sun, moon, and stars possibly reflect the astrological dynamics of most religions of the Roman world, especially the twelve stars, which could represent the zodiac.

It is something of the reality of God's inherent involvement in human history that the image of wisdom sought to portray; thus the identification of the woman with wisdom is not entirely wrong. The historical Incarnation of this reality of God came through Israel; thus the identification of the woman with Israel is not entirely wrong. The vision of New Jerusalem reveals that in some sense the city is God, thus the identification with the heavenly city is not entirely wrong. John's vision reveals that the church is in some way the continuing incarnation of God's self-giving in the world; thus the identification with the church is not entirely wrong. And since, in the historical particularity of the Incarnation, Jesus was born of the Virgin, the identification of the woman with Mary is not entirely wrong. Even the myths of Hellenistic religions may have seen through the glass darkly something of this profound mystery of God and thus helped prepare the way for the reality of John's vision.

The image of the woman with the wings of the great eagle adds weight to the suggestion that she is God. In the Song of Moses, God is imaged as the eagle who found Jacob in a desert land. In the howling waste of the wilderness, God, the eagle, encircled Jacob, cared for him, and kept him,

> "As an eagle stirs up its nest,
>   and hovers over its young;
> as it spreads its wings, takes them up,
>   and bears them on its pinions"
>   (Deuteronomy 32: 10-11).

In the Exodus account, God says to Moses, "I bore you on eagles' wings" (Exodus 19:4). The Psalmist sings in several places of the shadow of God's wings (Psalm 17:8; 36:7; 57:1; 63:7).

It would seem, therefore, that once again the vision images God as the woman. God, the Woman, has a "place" of nourishment in the midst of the "earth." Throughout the period of the dragon's realm (forty-two months/time, times, half-a-time), God is not weakened by the barrenness of the desert. This may represent the fact that not only can the dragon not overcome God in heaven, but it cannot overcome God in its own realm.

The Desert in Jewish Perspective
The desert or wilderness was the place where God would again reshape the covenant people (Hosea 2:14). This perspective developed into an eschatological expectation in Judaism, the belief that the last and decisive age of salvation will begin in the desert and that here the Messiah will appear.

Various messianic movements led people into the desert as the staging area for the victory of God (compare Acts 21:38 and the warning of Matthew 24:26). In the midst of the fall of Jerusalem in A.D. 70 with the Temple in flames, the Jews request the Romans to allow them to go into the desert.

8

Revelation
12:18–13:18

𝒜 BEASTLY TIME

Keep in mind the ways in which your class members learn best as you choose at least one learning activity from each of the three Dimensions.

Dimension 1:
What Does the Bible Say?

(A) Work with the study book questions.

1. Both images have seven heads and ten horns. The diadems, however, have moved from the heads on the dragon to the horns on the beast. In place of the diadems, the beast has a blasphemous name.

2. Be sure the class is aware of the impossible nature of the image of a mortal wound that was healed. *Mortal wound* and *healed* are mutually exclusive terms. John is obviously seeing something of such significance that this kind of *alert* is given to the readers.

Additional Discussion: Another way to approach the matter is to have the class members reflect on the most recent sporting event they have attended or watched. Ask:
—Can you identify the point in the contest where the final outcome became "set," the point at which the victory was

already won even though there may have been quite a bit of time remaining in the event?
—Did the losing team or individual walk out of the contest at that point? (Most likely not. Most likely the event continued to the end even though it was over earlier. It is something of this reality that the vision is conveying in the mortal wound that was healed.)

3. In comparing 16:13 and 19:20 one has a clearer understanding that the false prophet in each of these references is the beast from the earth in 13:11. Since the study book uses false prophet to designate the beast from the earth (13:11), from these other references the class members can see why this is legitimate.

4. Discuss what God is saying to Jeremiah in these passages, especially the nature of the people about whom the actions are spoken. (It should be noted that these actions are against those in opposition to God. This should confirm for the class that Revelation 13:10 does not apply to the saints but to the rebellious realm.)

Dimension 2:
What Does the Bible Mean?

(B) Make comparisons of the dragon and the beast.

- For this learning option you will need a large sheet of paper, pencil, and markers.
- If there is someone with artistic talent in the class, ask him or her to draw pictures of the dragon and the beast.
- Ask two class members to read aloud from Revelation, one person to read 12:3, another person to read 13:1.
- Provide a brief time for class members to compare the two images while one of the members writes the observations on a sheet of paper.
- Ask the class to discuss the material on this change found in the study book (pages 70-71).
- The primary focus of any discussion should focus on the blasphemous name, remembering that biblically *name* relates to the nature of the one named. Call the class's attention to the fact that this characteristic is highlighted again in the further description of the beast from the sea in 13:5-6.

(C) Study rebellion incarnate #1: the beast from the sea.

- For this learning option you will need large sheets of paper, markers, and tape, or chalkboard and chalk. Prior to class read in the Additional Bible Helps the article on "Daniel and the Beast" and "Daniel and Revelation."
- Give the class time to study Daniel 7:1-7, 17.
- Discuss the relationship between Daniel's vision and John's vision of the beast from the sea in 13:2. At this time make a list on a board or large sheet of paper of the attributes of Daniel's beasts and John's beast.
- During this discussion of the characteristics of Daniel's beasts and John's beast include information on Daniel's beasts from the Additional Bible Helps article.
- Have the class discuss the idea that John's beast is the archetype (an original model or type after which other things are patterned) that was incarnate in the four historical empires represented by Daniel's beasts.
- Include information from the Additional Bible Helps article, "Daniel and Revelation," to compare these two visions.
- Also discuss the new element in John's vision—that the beast has the dragon's power, throne, and great authority. This suggests that the beast is an incarnation in human existence of the rebellion of the dragon.

(D) Discover the importance of *forehead* and *right hand*.

- For this learning option you will need a concordance, paper, pens or pencils, and Bibles.
- Divide your class members into four groups and make the following assignments for each group.

Group One: Using a concordance look up the use of *forehead* in the Old Testament.

Group Two: Using a concordance look up the use of *right hand* in the Old Testament.

Ask the following question of these first two groups:
—What is the significance of these two images for people steeped in an Old Testament perspective?

Group Three: Look up the following references in the Book of Revelation—7:3; 9:4; 14:1; 22:4.

Discuss the significance of the image as it relates to the seal of God.

Group Four: Look up the following references in the Book of Revelation—13:6; 17:5; 20:4.

Discuss the significance of the image as it relates to the mark of the beast.

- Ask representatives from each group to report their findings.
- The important issue here is to realize that the images of "forehead" and "right hand" relate to the inner orientation of being and the outer behavior that results from that orientation.

(E) Talk about blasphemy.

- For this learning option you will need large sheets of paper, markers, and tape, or chalkboard and chalk. Review blasphemy from lesson 7.
- Have the class review the actions of the elders in Revelation 4:10. Discuss the meaning of these actions. (Their falling before the throne represents their acknowledgment of God as God. But even the demons make this acknowledgment—and shudder [James 2:19]. So, the elders also worship the one who lives for ever and ever. This is their willingness to allow God to be God, an acknowledgment of God's nature [or "name"] as God. As we saw in the previous lesson, however, it is possible for us to allow God to be God in our lives but on *our* terms. Thus, the elders also cast their crowns before the throne. This represents their willing acceptance of God's control over their lives, their desire to be those who dwell under God's purposes for their lives.)
- List these following three characteristics on the board or large sheet of paper:
—Acknowledge God as God
—Acknowledge God's name = Allow God to be God
—Submit to God's purposes
- Now have the class look at the blasphemies of the beast in Revelation 13:6.
- Ask:
—How do they relate to the actions of the elders? (It should be evident that the beast's blasphemy is the reversal of the elders's actions.)
- Remind the class that the beast has blasphemous names on its heads that indicate that its very nature is one of blas-

phemy toward God. This is the first aspect of the incarnation of the dragon's rebellion. The beast from the sea represents a posture of being that has no time or place for God in its outlook on life.

(F) Study the response to the beast.

- Divide the class members into two groups.
- Have **Group One** develop a list of all the appearances of "the inhabitants of the earth" in Revelation (3:10; 6:10; 8:13; 11:10; 13:8, 12, 14; 17:2, 8), indicating the various attributes or activities associated with this group.
NOTE: In 13:8, translations differ. The "inhabitants of the earth" (NRSV) can also be translated as those "whose name has not been written in the book of the life of the Lamb that was slain from the foundation of the world" (King James Version, New Jerusalem Bible) and "all who dwell on earth . . . every one whose name has not been written before the foundation of the world in the book of life of the Lamb that was slain" (Revised Standard Version).
- Have **Group Two** develop a list of all the appearances of the various combinations of "tribe and people and language and nation" (5:9; 7:9; 10:11; 11:9; 13:7; 14:6; 17:15), again noting the various attributes or activities of this group.
- Ask the groups to report their findings to the large group.
- Discuss the relationship of these two designations to Fallen Babylon and to New Jerusalem. Give special attention to the two places where the two expressions appear together (11:9-10 and 13:7-8).
NOTE: Two outcomes are desired in this exercise. First, the class should realize that both expressions are images for the citizens of Fallen Babylon who, as we see in this session, are under the authority of and worship the beast (13:7-8).

Second, the class should also realize that all the citizens of New Jerusalem were originally citizens of Fallen Babylon. They are now those who have been "ransomed for God *from* every tribe and language and people and nation" (5:9) and form that "great multitude that no one could count, *from* every nation, *from* all tribes and peoples and languages" (7:9). They have experienced this transfer of citizenship because they have "washed their robes and made them white in the blood of the Lamb" (7:14).

(G) Study rebellion incarnate #2: the beast from the earth.

Part One:

- To help the class members better understand the nature of the beast from the earth (the false prophet), read aloud the following section of Revelation 13. In the Scripture passage that follows each use of the Greek word *poieo*, meaning "to do, to make," is italicized in this NRSV translation. Take note what the beast from the earth does on behalf of the beast from the sea. As this passage is read

aloud, write on the board or the large sheet of paper the verbs that are from this Greek word (the italicized words).

[12]It *exercises* all the authority of the first beast on its behalf, and it *makes* the earth and its inhabitants worship the first beast, whose mortal wound had been healed. [13]It *performs* great signs, even *making* fire come down from heaven to earth in the sight of all; [14]and by the signs that it is allowed to *perform* on behalf of the beast, it deceives the inhabitants of earth, telling them to *make* an image for the beast that had been wounded by the sword and yet lived; [15]and it was allowed to give breath to the image of the beast so that the image of the beast could even speak and *cause* those who would not worship the image of the beast to be killed. [16]Also it *causes* all, both small and great, both rich and poor, both free and slave, to be marked on the right hand or the forehead.

- Have the class members discuss how the beast from the earth incarnates in action the blasphemous worldview of the beast from the sea.
- Discuss the attributes of this beast. Ask:
—Does the fact that this beast rises "from the earth" imply that it clothes itself in the structures humanity develops to shape its historical existence?
—Do the two horns like a lamb suggest that these structures are intended to be beneficial to humanity?
—Does the voice like the dragon imply that structures that are created to benefit human existence have a way of becoming demonic?

Part Two:

- Along this line, have the class brainstorm and develop a list of human organizations, agencies, or activities that were originated to benefit human welfare but have now become oppressive burdens on the backs of those whom they were intended to serve.
—Does the fact that the beast from the earth "makes" the inhabitants of the earth worship the beast from the sea indicate that an atmosphere of "political correctness" is characteristic of Fallen Babylon? In this connection, the class might consider the fact that the beast makes "war on the saints and conquers them" (13:7, 15) and does not allow those who refuse to worship the beast to have any part in the life of their politically correct world (13:17).
—Does this have any connection to the increasing hostility of various shapers of contemporary culture to the Christian worldview and lifestyle?
—Have the scientific and technological "miracles" of the past two centuries "deceived" humanity into idolizing the naturalistic humanism from which they came so that in our day there is little understanding of spiritual realities?

Dimension 3:
What Does the Bible Mean to Us?

(H) Study the mark of the beast.

WHAT'S IN A NUMBER?

The most prevalent modern solution is that the number of the mark of the beast represents Nero, the Roman emperor from A.D. 54 to 68, even though none of the fathers of the early church suggested this. The ancient world was entranced with a process known as *gematria*, whereby the letters of a person or object's name were changed into a numerical value and then added together to give the "number" of that person or object. There are two readings for the number in 13:18, one group of manuscripts has 666, the other 616. The name of Nero Caesar had two forms in the Roman Empire, the Greek form, Neron Caesar, and the Latin form, Nero Caesar. If both forms are transliterated into Hebrew letters, the value of Neron Caesar is 666, and the value of Nero Caesar is 616.

The question is whether John would have played with languages like this. He seems to do so in 9:11, where the name of the angel of the abyss is given in Hebrew and Greek. Since Hebrew and Greek are involved in the theory for 666, John may have given the clue to his readers in the two languages for the "name" of the angel of the abyss, expecting them to make the application to the mystery of the "name" of the beast. After all, it would not set well with Roman authorities to see the emperor identified as the incarnation of the beast.

It is very important to help the class realize that the number of the beast is not the significant element in the mark of the beast. The real focus is on the placement of the mark—on the forehead or the right hand.

- When we remember the significance of *forehead* and *right hand* in Dimension 2, activity (D), we can engage in some personal reflections on what this means for us. (The important issue is to realize that the images of "forehead" and "right hand" relate to the inner orientation of being and the outer behavior that results from that orientation.)
- Ask your class members to quietly reflect on the following questions:
—Are there areas of our lives where we have no time for God, no attentiveness to or interest in what God desires for us, areas where we exist with a perspective that does not acknowledge God, God's nature, or God's will? (John's vision reveals to us that in those areas of our lives, we have the mark of the beast upon our forehead.)
—Are there behaviors in our lives, such as habits, relationships, reactions to circumstances, ways of doing things that

are designed to enable us to retain control of our world and those in it? (Wherever such behaviors are present, there we have the mark of the beast upon our right hand.)
- Ask the class to reflect upon the fact that it is much "safer" to believe that the "mark of the beast" is something an autocratic world order is going to impose on everyone in the future than to face up to the fact that we may already carry that mark in our attitudes and behavior.

(I) You can't fight city hall.

John sees that the inhabitants of Fallen Babylon worship the beast because "Who is like the beast, and who can fight against it?" (13:4)
- For this learning option you will need large sheets of paper, tape, markers, or chalkboard and chalk.
- Have the class develop a list of situations in which they have heard others say, or have said themselves, that some Christian perspective or some Christian behavior just isn't realistic. Perhaps some biblical injunctions will help to trigger remembrance:
—Love your enemies (Matthew 5:44);
—Bless those who persecute you (Romans 12:14);
—If anyone has a legitimate complaint against another, forgive each other (Colossians 3:13);
—Rejoice always (Philippians 4:4);
—In everything give thanks (1 Thessalonians 5:18).
- Ask class members to divide into conversation groups and wrestle with whether our usual response to such injunctions reflects a mindset shaped more by Fallen Babylon than by New Jerusalem.

(J) Identify the voices of the dragon.

- For this learning option you will need large sheets of paper, markers, and tape, or chalkboard and chalk. Also you will need small sheets of paper, pencils, or pens.
- Develop with the entire class a list of those "voices" that powerfully shape the worldview and lifestyle of our culture, "voices" that in light of John's vision, are really the voice of the dragon in our day. Write these "voices" on the chalkboard or large paper. (Some of these voices are obvious: those who advocate violence as the answer to any perceived injustice; those who pornographically exploit women and children; those who denigrate the family. Other "voices" are so subtle that we don't hear the dragon's accent in them: the voices of consumerism, of acquisitiveness, of entitlement, of materialism.)
NOTE: This should not be an exercise in labeling those with whom we disagree as voices of the dragon. This should be an exercise in analyzing the voices we hear and heed in our own daily lives. Let anyone who has an ear listen!
- After you have made a list and have had discussion on the presence of these "voices" in our culture, hand out paper and pens or pencils to each class member.

- In a quiet time of reflection ask each class member to select and write on her or his paper a "voice" that they most struggle against.
- Then ask each person to write down three ways that he or she will be more attuned to this "voice" and thus be able to withstand the temptation it offers.
- Challenge class members this week to make a change in the way(s) they are lured by the "voice."

Additional Bible Helps

Daniel and the Beast

The power of the beast is manifest through the vision's modulation of Daniel's vision of four beasts from the sea, three of which were a leopard, bear, and lion (Daniel 7:1-7). Daniel saw the representatives of four world empires that exercised control over Palestine and the Jewish people (*Babylon*: the lion with eagle's wings; *Persia*: the bear; *Alexander the Great's empire*: the leopard with four wings [representing Alexander's four generals who divided his realm among themselves when he died]; and the *Seleucid dynasty*: the terrible beast, its ten horns representing a succession of kings in the Seleucid dynasty and the arrogant little horn representing Antiochus Epiphanes who attempted to eradicate the Jewish faith from Palestine [Daniel 7:21]).

The combination of attributes of Daniel's beasts in comparison to the one beast in John's vision suggests that Daniel's beasts were four partial and historical manifestations of the single beast that John sees. The beast of John's vision is the deeper reality behind the beasts of Daniel's vision. The focus on the mouth of the beast emphasizes its role in the beast's blasphemy; its appearance as a lion's mouth may suggest its attempt to imitate the Lion of Judah in the same manner that the second beast attempts to imitate a lamb but speaks like a dragon (13:11).

Daniel and Revelation

Many interpretations of Revelation incorporate the Book of Daniel into their interpretative scheme. It is obvious that John employed a number of images from Daniel to convey his visionary experience. As we see in this session, Daniel's vision of the four beasts from the sea have been adapted and modified by John to convey his vision of the beast from the sea. The very fact that John has modulated Daniel's imagery should alert us to the fact that Daniel is not the interpretive guide to Revelation. There are two basic reasons why Daniel is not the basis for interpreting Revelation.

First, Daniel's vision is not dealing with God's purposes in human history in the same way as John's vision. Daniel's visions are, essentially, insights into the history of the Jewish people from the time of the Babylonian captivity (587 B.C.) down to the Maccabean revolution (167-162 B.C.). What is often taken as Daniel's vision of end times is, in reality, his vision of the future deliverance of God in the Messiah.

Daniel, therefore, is a vision leading up to the coming of the Messiah.

Second, John's vision is "the revelation of Jesus Christ" (1:1). John is seeing what God has done, is doing, and will do in Christ. In a sense, John's vision picks up where Daniel's leaves off. Daniel's vision is as far as the coming of Christ; John's vision is from Christ on. John, therefore, is able to operate from a completely different frame of reference than Daniel. John knows the historical manifestation of God in Christ whereas Daniel could only see through a glass darkly.

More Than an Image

The Jews and early Christians regarded with horror images of gods and prohibited any kind of representation of God. What is involved in the "image" of the beast, however, is the broader understanding of *image* itself.

In the Hellenistic world of the Roman Empire, with its tremendous diversity of divinities and its even greater proliferation of their images, the term *image* had a significant meaning. An image was not merely an artistic representation of the god, but an *incarnation of the god*. The image partook of the reality of that which it imaged. Something of this use can be seen in Paul when he writes that Christ "is the image of the invisible God" (Colossians 1:15). Therefore *image* does not imply something less than whatever it is a likeness of. Rather it implies the clarification or enlightenment of its essence. In the image we somehow have God present in our own being.

Coming from the Jewish frame of reference, an *idol* is not an incarnation of a reality. It has no reality behind it at all. An idol is *an empty thing*. An idol is not merely a choice between something else and God or a choice of something else instead of God; it is an illusory or insubstantial god, and therefore false, not true or real. Throughout the vision John seems to make this distinction between *idol* and *image*. The vision presents idolatry, along with a catalog of other vices, as one of the consequences of values, structures, and dynamics that "image" the blasphemy of the beast. It seems unlikely, therefore, that idolatry is involved in the image of the beast.

Triple Images

The image of the number of the beast can be interpreted in more than one way. The complex imagery in the vision allows for other dimensions in the number of the beast. There are three triads in the vision: holy, holy, holy (4:8); woe, woe, woe (8:13); and six, six, six (13:18). The triad of the nature of God could be contrasted with the triad of the nature of the beast, with the woes being the result of the encounter between the two.

Again, the number six represented imperfection or incompletion in the same way that the numbers three and seven represented perfection or totality. The nature of the beast, therefore, is the "perfect" (triple) imperfection (sixes). This could be related to the fact that the rebellion resulted in the loss of a "third" (.333) from the created order. The imperfection that remains is two-thirds (.666).

9

Revelation 14:1–15:8

Good News, Bad News, You Choose

LEARNING MENU

Keep in mind the ways in which your class members learn best as you choose at least one learning activity from each of the three Dimensions.

Dimension 1: What Does the Bible Say?

(A) Work with the study book questions

1. Fearing God is the willing acknowledgement of God being God and a willing submission of one's life to God. This kind of fear of God is what the elders express when they bow before the One who sits on the throne.

2. The endurance that is referred to in the vision (1:9; 2:2, 3, 19; 3:10; 13:10; 14:12) is one that speaks to the relationship between God and those who are struggling to be faithful. The world (Fallen Babylon) does not value or support this relationship with God.

3. One way to look at the parallel terms or phrases in this passage about the harvest (Revelation 14:14-20) would be by putting this passage on the board or on a large sheet of paper in a way that would highlight the parallelism between 14:14-16 and 17-20.

If time is short, prepare this assignment in advance and bring it in for the class. It will then be helpful as the class discusses the vision of the harvest.

The comparison would look something like this:

14:14-16	14:17-20
seated on a white cloud was one like the Son of Man golden crown on his head sharp sickle in his hand	Another angel came out of the temple in heaven had a sharp sickle
An angel came out of the temple calling: "Use your sickle and reap. . . .the harvest of the earth is completely ripe."	Another angel came from the altar (the angel who has authority over fire) calls to the one with the sharp sickle "Use your sharp sickle and gather the clusters of the vine of the earth, for its grapes are ripe."
So [Christ] puts his sickle *upon* [NRSV "over"] the earth, and the earth was reaped.	So the angel swung his sickle *into* [NRSV "over"] the earth (The sickle that gathers the rebellious is put forth "into" the earth. This is one of those series of things that go "into" the earth. "Into" the earth represents the consequence of the presence of God in the rebellious order.)
	The angel throws the grapes into the wine press of the wrath of God.
	The wine press was trodden outside the city, blood flowed from the wine press. . .

(B) Fear God!

- For this learning option you will need large sheets of paper, markers, and tape, or chalkboard and chalk.
- Ask for a quick response to the following question:
—What comes to your mind when you hear the phrase *fear God*?
- Write the list of responses on a board or large sheet of paper for future reference.
- Presuming that the class has reviewed the role of fearing God in the vision (study book question 1, Dimension 1), divide them into three or four groups and have each group study the role of fearing God in a section of the Old Testament. References can be added by using a concordance. But here are some Scripture passages to get the groups started: Genesis 15:1; 20:11; 42:18; Exodus 9:30; 20:20; Deuteronomy 4:10; 6:13; 17:13; 17:19; Psalm 2:11; 33:8; 85:9; Proverbs 9:10; 14:27; 15:33; 22:4; Isaiah 33:6; Jeremiah 5:24.
- Have the small groups develop a list of the aspects of fearing God that they have developed from their study of the Old Testament passages.
- Have each group give their findings and insights in the large group. Record these findings on paper or on the chalkboard.
(Focus the exercise on what the idea of fearing God reveals about the nature of human relationship with God.)
- Compare the biblical list with the original list developed by the class members at the beginning.
- Have the class reflect upon what their list reveals about their understanding of relationship with God.
- Discuss why the evangelistic call to the citizens of Fallen Babylon ("those who live on the earth—to every nation and tribe and language and people"—14:6) is "Fear God."
NOTE: The object of this exercise is to help the class realize another dimension of the radical nature of relationship with God. According to the vision, fearing God is the deep inner reorientation of our being toward God that brings about our transfer of citizenship from Fallen Babylon to New Jerusalem.

(C) Associate first fruits with relationship to God.

- For this learning option you will need Bibles, concordance, Bible dictionary, paper, pens or pencils.
- Also prior to class time read the article in Additional Bible Helps on "First Fruits." Include information from this article during the discussion when appropriate.

- Divide your class into three groups and make the following assignments:
Group One: Study some of the references to first fruits in the Old Testament. Ask:
—What role did the first fruits play in Israel's relationship with God? (Jeremiah 2:3).
Group Two: Study the role of the Levites in the Old Testament. Begin with Numbers 3. (Also this group might want to consult a Bible dictionary.)
Group Three: Study the images of first fruits in the New Testament.
- After allowing about ten minutes for research, ask that each group report its findings to the whole class.
- With this work as reference, have the class discuss the image of first fruit applied to those who are with the Lamb on Mount Zion in 14:1-5.
NOTE: The object of this exercise is for the participants to realize the radical nature of the relationship with God that is being imaged in John's vision. As the first fruits, the Levites were totally consecrated to God and their lives devoted to God's service. All the other images of the followers of the Lamb—undefiled, virgins, no lie in their mouth, blameless—serve to heighten the depths of devotion to God that are expected of the followers of the Lamb.

(D) What is the real situation?

- Remind the class that up to this point in this portion of the vision, things don't look so good for the citizens of New Jerusalem. Their Messiah is snatched out of the mouth of the dragon (12:5); the dragon has declared war upon them (12:17); the beast from the sea makes war against them and conquers them (13:7); they are killed because they don't worship the image of the beast (13:15); and without the mark of the beast on their forehead or right hand they cannot participate in the affairs of normal life (13:17). There doesn't seem to be much to commend New Jerusalem citizenship as a viable option. The call for the endurance of the saints in the midst of all this (13:10) certainly seems to be an understatement!
- For this learning option you will need a Bible dictionary, concordance, leader's guide information on 144,000 (session five), a commentary on the Book of Revelation, paper, pens or pencils.
- Divide your class members into three groups.
Group One: Review the role of 144,000 in the vision. Compare activity (E) in session 5.
Group Two: Use a concordance to study the role of Zion and Mount Zion in the Old Testament. Ask them to be especially alert to the prophetic visions of the role of Zion and Mount Zion in God's future kingdom.
Group Three: Look at Revelation 14:1. (This group might want to consult a commentary on Revelation for additional information and to look up Hebrews 12:22. Mount Zion

appears elsewhere in the New Testament only in Hebrews 12:22.)

- After allowing about ten minutes for research, ask the groups to report their findings to the whole class.
- With all this information before the class, ask them to look at the perspective on how the Christian movement understood its relationship to the Old Testament expectations.
- With this background discuss the force of the image of Mount Zion in John's vision. (The outcome of this should be a realization that although John's readers found themselves a marginalized and persecuted minority in their Fallen Babylon world of first century Rome, they were participants in the fulfillment of God's promised kingdom.)

(E) Take a close look at the name.

- For this learning option you will need a large sheet of paper or white posterboard, markers, crayons, various colors of construction paper or tissue paper, scissors, glue, glitter, and tape. Also you will need a chalkboard or other sheets of paper upon which to record general ideas.
- Prior to class ask a class member who has artistic skills to draw off on the posterboard or large sheet of paper a coat of arms shield. Divide the shield into five different sections.

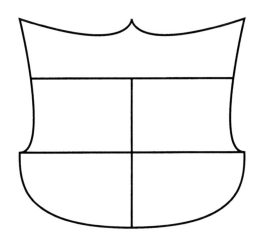

Part One:
- Note how the vision of God's redeemed with the name of God and the Lamb on their foreheads follows immediately upon the vision of those who have the mark of the beast (or the name of the beast—13:17) on their forehead. This is one of the clear images of contrast between the two orders of being available for human existence.
- Ask the class members to name the qualities of those who have the name of God and the Lamb on their foreheads as revealed in 14:4-5, and what they reveal about Christian discipleship. Record these ideas on large paper or chalkboard. Include the following information in the discussion:

—*Have not defiled themselves with women* and *virgins*. Since celibacy was not a characteristic either of Judaism or early Christianity, the vision is most likely using sexual imagery in conjunction with spiritual fornication. The disciples have not adulterated their relationship with the Lamb. If there is time, the class could look at the usages of sexual imagery for spiritual debasement in the vision. It is also significant that the focal image of the rebellious order, is presented as a whore (17:1).

—*Follow the Lamb wherever he goes*. This would appear to be an image of radical obedience, especially when the Lamb is introduced as slain (5:6), even from the foundation of the world (13:8).

—*Have been redeemed from humankind as first fruits*. Refer to the discussion in Dimension 2, activity (C).

—*Have no lie in their mouth*. Lying seems to be one of the consistent characteristics of the citizens of Fallen Babylon (compare also 21:27 and 22:15).

—*Are blameless*. An interesting characteristic in that it appears only here in Revelation. Elsewhere in the New Testament, however, it is used for a state of perfect relationship with God, appearing almost exclusively in Paul's writings.

- After you have listed these five qualities of those who have the name of God and the Lamb on their forehead, you may want to put these ideas into artistic representations. If so, continue in Part Two.

Part Two:
- Using the previously discussed ideas about the qualities of those who have the name of God and the Lamb on their forehead as components of Christian discipleship, divide your class members into five groups—one for each of the characteristics listed above.
- Ask each small group to reflect on the meaning of its characteristic. If there are additional Scripture passages listed above, supply these to the appropiate group.
- After the small group discussions ask the groups to think of an appropriate symbol to represent their characteristic.
- Show the groups the shield drawn on the posterboard. If your class is not familiar with coat of arms, share the information in the Teaching Tip box (page 48).
- Supply groups with art materials and ask them to put their symbol on the shield.
- Leave your class creation displayed for the rest of the study on Revelation as a reminder of the components of Christian discipleship.

(F) Study and illustrate the concept of harvest time.

- For this learning option you will need a large sheet of paper, markers, tape, paper, and pens or pencils. Also read in the Additional Bible Helps the article, "Who Harvests Whom," and be prepared to include this information in your discussion.

- Tell the class that the harvest image for the consummation of God's purposes is common in both the Old and New Testaments. Then have the class members divide into two groups and give each group one of the harvest images (grain/grapes, Son of man/angels).

- Ask each group to read Revelation 14:14-20.

- Ask them to note the characteristics of the image in each place, especially noting who harvests whom.

- Encourage each group to look up other Old Testament and New Testament usages for their harvest images. (Some examples include *grain*—Isaiah 27:12; Joel 3:13; Matthew 3:12; *grapes*—Isaiah 63:3; Lamentations 1:15; Joel 3:13; *Son of man*—Daniel 7:13; Matthew 13:41; 25:31; Mark 8:38; Luke 9:26; 12:8-9; *angels*—Matthew 13:39; 13:49; 2 Thessalonians 1:7; Mark 13:27.)

- Ask each group to report to the whole class. Record findings in chart form on the chalkboard or large paper.

- To carry the discussion one step further, bring out the chart of the parallel structure of 14:14-20 that was developed under Dimension 1, activity (A), question 3.

- In the parallel structure of the two sides of the harvest, note that the Son of man figure harvests a grain crop (the Greek behind *fully ripe* means "dried out"), a common image of gathering God's people into God's granary (Matthew 13:30; Luke 3:17). The angelic harvester gathers grapes for the wine press, a common image for judgment of the wicked (Isaiah 63:2-3; Lamentations 1:15; Joel 3:13).

(G) How is *endurance* part of the relationship with God?

- If there are enough members in the class, assign each of the seven occurrences of *endurance* in Revelation (1:9; 2:2, 3, 19; 3:10; 13:10; 14:12) to a different person or group of persons.

- Ask them to reflect more fully on how the word functions in its context.

- Have the class clarify the situations in which endurance is practiced in the vision.

- Ask:

—Do you think there is any significance that *endurance* is one of the lists of things that appear seven times in the vision?

—What light does *endurance* shed upon the nature of faithful relationship with God in a Fallen Babylon world?

NOTE: The purpose of this experience is to highlight the "other side" of relationship with God. This exercise focuses upon how that relationship plays itself out in a world that does not value such a relationship.

(H) Good news? Bad news? You choose.

- Have the class discuss the material in the study book on this section (14:6-12), pages 82-84.

- Note that immediately after the sharp contrast between those who have the name of the beast on their forehead with those who have the name of God and the Lamb, the vision shows the offer of transformation to the citizens of Fallen Babylon.

- Show visually how all the images of Fallen Babylon are drawn together in these few verses:

Good News:	"those who live on the earth—to every nation and tribe and language and people" (6)
Bad News:	"fallen, fallen is Babylon the Great" (8)
You Choose:	"those who worship the beast and its image and . . . anyone who receives the mark of its name" (9)

- Point out to the class the significance of the conditional structure of the "You Choose" section (14:9-11). (One can either "fear God and give him glory. . . .and worship him who made heaven and earth," or one can "worship the beast and its image" and receive "the mark." Even in a strong image of the judgment of Fallen Babylon, there is the reminder that no one need experience the torment of that judgment. It is only if one continues to choose to wor-

ship the beast and receive its name that she or he will experience the inevitable consequences of that choice.)
● Ask:
—How do these choices continue to be available to us?

(I) How can we love our enemies?

● Have the class develop what they believe a Christian response should be to a world that abuses and destroys them.
● For this learning option you will need several current newspapers or news magazines, scissors, glue, paper, and markers.
● Divide class members into several small groups. Distribute the newspapers or news magazines. Instruct the small groups to look for examples of brokenness in the world—crime, killing, abuse. Then cut out these examples from the newspapers, glue them on paper, and give a title to the event from the victim's perspective.
● Tape these up around your classroom.
● Then challenge your class members to think of a response from the Christian perspective. Share these ideas.
● Ask:
—What insights are presented in John's vision? (One might expect that the Christian response to persecution and death at the hands of the Fallen Babylon world would be at least an aloofness if not outright hostility to that world that treated them so. Instead John's vision next sees the proclamation of the gospel to Fallen Babylon. This is wonderfully consistent with God's relationship with the fallen realm. Even though the unchanging holiness of God burns inexorably against the destructive brokenness of the rebellion, all of God's actions are aimed at bringing that realm to repentance and life. This is seen in the repeated remark, "they did not repent" [9:20-21; 16:9, 11].)
—What does all this seem to mean for us?
   (As disciples of Christ we should be persons of such deep, abiding joy that our lives, even in the face of opposition, persecution, and death, are to the world winsome witnesses of a realm of being of wholeness and transforming power.)
● Discuss with your class members the challenges and struggles in offering the love of Christ in a broken world.

(J) Sing a new song.

● If you choose to have the class work with this learning option, take some time to have the class share with each other whether joy and singing are vital parts of their perspective of Christian experience.
● Then have the class answer the same question in the context of John's vision of Christian experience in a Fallen Babylon world. In John's vision Christians are being persecuted and martyred. In addition, John's vision, as we have seen, reveals Christian discipleship in rigorous terms.
● Ask for several volunteers to engage in imaginative role-

playing in which the class members would understand themselves to be marginalized, ostracized, hounded, or persecuted, with some of their brothers and sisters having been martyred for the faith. Allow them several minutes to get their roleplay together. Share their ideas with the whole class.
● Add to that imagination a call for a radical consecration of one's total life to God. Remembering the repeated calls to "endurance" in John's vision might assist this imaginative exercise.
● Ask:
—Would you now see joy and singing as a vital part of Christian experience?
● Ask the class to think about the following examples:
   (1) Consider Paul's injunction to "rejoice in the Lord always" (Philippians 4:4). Here is a man sitting in a Roman dungeon, not knowing whether he will ever get out alive. In Philippians 2:17-18, Paul says, "But even if I am being poured out as a libation over the sacrifice and the offering of your faith, I am glad and rejoice with all of you—and in the same way you also must be glad and rejoice with me." (Either the man is a lunatic of the first order, or he has learned a secret of Christian life that would benefit all.)
   (2) In John's vision of the redeemed with the Lamb (14:1-5), the new song is at the center of the picture. It could remind one of Paul and Silas sitting in the Philippian prison at midnight, their backs bloodied from the rods, their feet locked in stocks, singing and praising God (Acts 16:16-25).
● Point out that John's vision is explicit in its observation that only the redeemed know this song. It seems that we are seeing here a profound dimension of life in relationship with God. We see a wholeness and integrity of being, a deep inner strength, that enables Christian disciples to face even death with equanimity.
● An appropriate ending for this learning option would be to close by singing a hymn. Two suggestions from *The United Methodist Hymnal* are "For All the Saints" (711) and "Holy, Holy, Holy! Lord God Almighty" (64).

Additional Bible Helps

First Fruits
One dimension of the "first fruits" image relates to the Jewish festival of first fruits, the Feast of Weeks, also known as Pentecost (Exodus 34:22; Leviticus 23:15; Deuteronomy 16:9-12). At least for the early church, with the remembrance of the Pentecost experience of the Holy Spirit, which brought into being a new people of God, the image would have deep overtones for their citizenship in New Jerusalem. Something of the same dimensions are brought out by Paul when he reminds the Roman Christians that they have the first fruits of the Holy Spirit (Romans 8:23).

The "first fruit" image applied to Christians is not exclusive to John's vision. James tells his readers, "[God] gave us birth by the word of truth, so that we would become a kind of first fruits of [God's] creatures" (James 1:18). If the saints are the first fruits, then the vision implies that they serve God in the Temple on behalf of the rest of humanity.

Who's Afraid?

Fear of God in the Old Testament, while at times expressing the terror of humans at the awesome power of God and the deadly danger of God's holiness, more often signifies the reverence and submission due to God as God. This is seen especially in the Wisdom tradition. In Proverbs, fear of Yahweh is the knowledge of God (Proverbs 2:5). The same formula is found in the parallel phrases in Proverbs 9:10.

The fear of God, then, is not the coercive fear of a tyrant, but the willing acknowledgment of God being God and a submission of one's life to the godhood of God. This kind of fear of God is what the elders express when they bow before the One who sits upon the throne.

Who Harvests Whom?

The image of the Son of man sitting upon the cloud recalls Daniel 7:13 and following. In Daniel, however, the image has nothing to do with the final harvest of the earth but with the eternal dominion of the Son of man figure. But the image of the Son of man coming on the clouds in the final harvest of the earth, especially in conjunction with angels, does have antecedents in the teachings of Jesus as well as the other New Testament writings.

It appears first on the lips of Jesus, "Those who are ashamed of me and of my words in this adulterous and sinful generation, of them the Son of Man will also be ashamed when he comes in the glory of his Father with the holy angels" (Mark 8:38; Luke 9:26; compare Matthew 25:31; Luke 12:8-9). This image is further developed in Matthew 16:27: "The Son of Man is to come with his angels in the glory of his Father, and then he will repay everyone for what has been done." Here the idea of a separation of persons into two groups is intimated. The intimation becomes clear in Matthew 13:41 where Jesus teaches, "The Son of Man will send his angels, and they will collect out of his kingdom all causes of sin and all evildoers, and they will throw them into the furnace of fire" (compare Matthew 13:49 and 2 Thessalonians 1:7). Just prior to this teaching, in the explanation of the parable, Jesus had said that the harvesters were angels (Matthew 13:39). Thus the image of harvest is also joined to the image of the Son of man and angels. In Matthew 24:31, the Son of man who comes on clouds "will send out his angels . . . and they will gather his elect from the four winds" (compare Mark 13:27).

It would appear that the image of Christ as the Son of man figure coming with angels to inaugurate the final consummation of God's purposes was a common expectation in the early church. What John sees, therefore, is Christ and the angels engaged in this consummation of God's purposes.

As seen in Jesus' explanation of the parable, harvesting was an image for the fulfillment of God's purposes. Perhaps an antecedent of the reality of John's vision was seen by Joel who prophesied

> "Put in the sickle,
>   for the harvest is ripe.
> Go in, tread,
>   for the wine press is full" (3:13).

Two harvests are implied in Joel. One is the harvest of grass-type crops (wheat, barley, and so forth), which are gathered with a sickle; the other, the harvest of the vines, which is trodden in a wine press. The same two harvests are seen in John's vision. The harvest of grapes is obvious in 14:18-20, but the harvest of grass-type crops in 14:15-16 is not so clear. It is found in the words for *ripe* and *harvest*. The word for *ripe* in 14:15, means "dry," that is, grain crops that have come to the point of dryness for harvest. The term for *harvest* means "to reap a grain-type crop."

Throughout the Bible, the image of reaping the grain-type crop is used to portray God's gathering in of the faithful. Also, the image of treading the winepress is used to portray God's judgment upon the rebellious. The vision employs images that resonate deeply with John and his readers. They would realize that Christ is gathering the citizens of New Jerusalem, and the angel is gathering the citizens of Fallen Babylon.

10

Revelation 15:5–16:21

REDEMPTIVE WRATH

Dimension 1:
What Does the Bible Say?

(A) Work with the study book questions.

1. As the class considers each appearance of *plague* in John's vision, the object here is to realize that the presence of God's holiness is a "plague" to Fallen Babylon and all its citizens from the dragon (13:3) to its subjects (16:2, 9).

Additional Discussion: Have the class sort the uses of *plague* into those that affect the citizens of New Jerusalem and those that affect the citizens of Fallen Babylon.

2. Discuss the apparent peculiarity of the presence of repentance in the midst of the bowls of the "wrath" of God. The object here is to begin to realize that God's "wrath" is not meant for the destruction of the fallen realm but for its repentance and liberation from its destructive bondage.

Additional Discussion: You could begin discussion of this question by having the class share what the word *repent* means to them. List on a chalkboard or large sheet of paper the diversity of perspectives.

● Then divide your class members into two groups. Ask one group to study the use of *repent* in relation to Christians (chapters 2–3) and the other its use in relation to the citizens of Fallen Babylon).

● If two groups are used, have them share their perspectives with each other and compare what they found in Revelation with the list they developed at the start of the exercise.

3. Many scholars think that the seven bowls with the seven trumpets are variants. Remind the class of the difference between the trumpets and bowls. (The first four trumpets seem to apply to all human existence since the last three are specifically designated for the people of Fallen Babylon. The first four bowls, by contrast, are specifically focused upon the citizens of the dragon's realm.)

Have the class consider whether the bowls might be a deeper revelation of what the trumpets introduce. Could the trumpets reveal the broader parameters of the rebellion and its consequences and the bowls narrow that focus down to the fallen realm?

(B) Take a closer look at the golden vessels.

• Divide your class members into three small groups. Each group will study references to golden vessels.

Group One:

• Study the golden vessels in John's vision (5:8; 8:3 and 5; 15:7).

• Consider the following question:

—What connection might there be between the golden censer poured into the earth in 8:5 and the golden bowls poured into the earth in chapter 16?

Group Two:

• Look up these Scriptures: Revelation 1:12, 20; 2:1; 21:23.

• Consider the symbolism of the golden lampstands in John's vision (1:12, 20; 2:1). Ask:

—Do you think the golden lampstands could be another golden "vessel," in a manner of speaking? (Later in the vision John sees that New Jerusalem needs no sun for light by day nor moon by night because God's presence is its light [21:23]. In that same place, John also sees that the lamp for that light is the Lamb! This brings a whole new perspective on the image of the churches as lampstands. The lamp they hold is the Lamb!)

Group Three:

• Read Revelation 17:4.

• There is one golden vessel associated with Fallen Babylon. Ask:

—In what way is the whore associated with being a golden vessel? (The whore has "a golden cup full of abominations and the impurities of her fornication" [17:4].)

• After you have allowed about five minutes for the groups to look up their Scripture passages and think about their questions, ask them to share their findings with the whole group.

• Discuss any possible connections that the class sees between these golden vessels. Here are some of the possible options:

—Since the prayers of the saints are associated with the golden bowls of the elders and of the angel in the seventh seal, and since such prayer is implied to take place within the life of the churches (review the role of the "angel" of the church in session 2 of the study book), is it possible that the golden bowls are simply a variation of the golden lampstands?

—Since the prayers of the saints are poured out of the golden censer of the angel in the seventh seal into the fallen order ("the earth") and the result is the disruptive presence of God in the midst of that order ("peals of

thunder, rumblings, flashes of lightning, and an earthquake"), could this be one of the consequences of the church holding forth in the world the Lamb, the lamp of the light of God?

—Since golden bowls are first associated with the prayers of the saints (5:8), and the prayers of the saints appear to be the means of the release of God's presence into the world, could the golden bowls of the "wrath" of God be describing more completely the consequences of the angels' action in the seventh seal? (The imagery of the bowls of wrath at least shows the profound disruption of the dragon's realm by God's presence in its midst.)

(C) Study the wrath of God.

• For this learning option you will need a concordance, large sheets of paper, markers, and tape, or chalkboard and chalk.

• Have the class members develop a list of adjectives that help them clarify the wrath of God. For instance, someone might think of the punitive wrath of God, another might choose vengeful, and so on. Write these on the chalkboard or large paper.

• Have a concordance available for the class, and ask someone to report on how many appearances of *wrath* there are in the Old Testament as compared with the New Testament. (A quick computer run on the NRSV indicates over six times as many in the Old Testament as in the New. A computer search of the Greek NT reveals 36 uses).

• Another person might report on the distribution of the New Testament uses of *wrath*. (Of the total number of New Testament uses, 13 are in Revelation and 20 in four letters of Paul—with 12 of those in Romans. Only 4 are in the Gospels, and two of those are a parallel, Matthew 3:7 and Luke 3:7.)

• Have the class reflect upon the obvious fact that *wrath* is not a major aspect of God in the New Testament and especially not in the ministry of Jesus. (These statistics might lead the class to do a more in-depth study of *wrath* in the New Testament.)

• Above all, have the class members give consideration to the idea that the *wrath* of God is the love of God that burns against all that is destructive to God's beloved creation.

• You might want to use the following illustration in clarifying this point:
Have the class imagine themselves meeting, for some strange reason, on the highest point of the church's building. When the class is over, certain members of the class decide that climbing down by whatever means got them up there is too slow. They decide to simply step off from where they are.

• Ask:

—Does the law of gravity suddenly become punitive, vindictive, vengeful, retributive (and all the other adjectives the class developed above)? Up to this point the law of gravity has been friendly.

—Does it suddenly become mean? (Of course not! The law of gravity simply keeps on being what it has always been.)

• Explain that God is certainly not an impersonal "force" like gravity, but the principle holds. God doesn't suddenly become punitive, vindictive, vengeful, retributive, or mean when God's created persons rebel against God. God simply continues to be God. The persons who step off the high point of the church don't break the law of gravity. They break themselves against it.

• Ask:
—Could the same be true of God? (We don't break the "laws" of our wholeness, which structure our relationship with God; we break ourselves against them. This breaking is painful, disruptive, debilitating, and ultimately destructive.)

• Discuss whether this could be the reason why the notes about repenting appear in the middle of the bowls of wrath. If the "wrath" were designed to be punitive, vindictive, vengeful, retributive, or mean, repentance would be the last thing desired. The desire would be to extract the last drop of satisfaction in the torment of the victim.

• It should also be noted that the note on repentance appears in a similar setting in 9:20-21.

(D) Consider *Armageddon.*

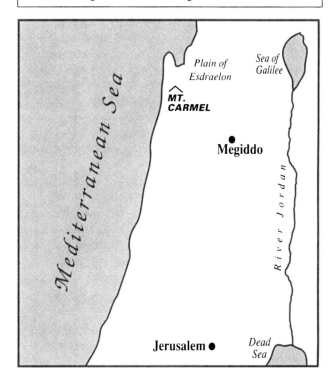

• Prior to class time be familiar with the information in the above box, as well as the information given in the study book on Armageddon, page 94. Begin this learning option by reviewing the information in the study book and with the class members; add the above information in the discussion. Be sure to include that the *exact place* referred to in Revelation is not the main point, rather that the place represents the place where God and the powers opposed to God encounter.

• Ask a class member to read aloud 16:12-16.

• Point out to the class how the blessing in 16:15, intrudes into the middle of the description of the gathering of the forces of rebellion. One way to do this is to have everyone close their Bibles and then read for them 16:14 and 16. Ask them if they notice anything missing.

• Then discuss why the blessing is "inserted" as it is. (It appears that one purpose is to emphasize that the followers of the Lamb are right in the center of this mobilization of the forces of rebellion against God.)

• Have the class look ahead to 20:9 where the "camp of the saints" is again at the center of the mobilization of the forces of the rebellion. Obviously the community of God's people are very much at the center of the rebellious order's warfare with God.

- Ask:
—Is John seeing another aspect of the dragon's war against "the rest of the (woman's) children, those who keep the commandments of God and hold the testimony of Jesus" (12:17)?

(E) Discuss blasphemy and God's response to it.

- Ask a class member to read aloud 13:6. Discuss what is happening in this verse. (In 13:6 the beast blasphemed God, God's name, and God's dwelling that was defined as "those who dwell in heaven." This is the rebellious order's *negative worship of God*, the polar opposite of the elders who bow before God, worship God, and cast their crowns before the throne.)
- Ask another class member to read aloud 16:9, 11, 21.
- Ask:
—Do you see a similarity with 13:6? (It is interesting to note that the rebellious order's response to the bowls of wrath repeats the same three blasphemies, although in different sequence. First, in 16:9, "they cursed ['blasphemed' in the Greek] the name of God." Second, in 16:11, they "cursed the God of heaven." Finally, in 16:21, "they cursed God.")
- Then discuss God's response to those who blaspheme. (God does not remove God's self from those that blaspheme God. Rather God continues to place God's self and the people of the New Jerusalem in their midst. God does not wish for the broken relationship to continue. God desires all the created order to be in relationship with God.)

Dimension 3: What Does the Bible Mean to Us?

(F) Holiness is a serious matter.

- Resources and supplies needed for this learning option are Bible commentaries on Exodus, 1 Kings, Psalms, and Revelation, Bible dictionary, paper, pens or pencils.
- Divide the class members into two research groups. Tell the class that one of the many puzzles of Revelation is the image of the Temple filled with smoke that no one can enter until the seven plagues are ended (15:5-8).
- Ask a class member to read this passage aloud.

Group One:
- Ask this group to research the image of smoke related to God's glory. Some passages to look at include the following: Exodus 40:34-35; 1 Kings 8:10-11; and Psalm 18:6-11. One could consider these passages as possible preceding events and images for John's image.
- If time and resources allow, obtain a Bible commentary and study the comments on these passages.

Group Two:
- Ask this group to do a study of the "glory" of God. The Greek term for *glory* is *dovxh* (*doxe*, from which we get our word *doxology*). A person's "glory" is that quality of their inner being that makes them who they are. In a word, "glory" is a reference to the essence of the person. Thus, to speak of God's "glory" is to refer to the very nature of God's being. Several Scripture passages to study include 2 Corinthians 3:17-18: "And all of us, with unveiled faces, seeing the glory of the Lord . . . are being transformed into the same image from one degree of glory to another" (literally, in Greek, "from glory into glory"). Paul is speaking here of the transformation of our beings into the likeness of Christ from what we are in our brokenness and incompleteness ("from glory") to what Christ is in the fulness of his being ("into glory"). Another Scripture to look up is Romans 5:2 where Paul states clearly, "We boast in our hope of sharing the glory of God."
- This group also might want to look up "glory" in a Bible dictionary for more information.
- In the presentation of their findings to the whole class, this group might also want to sing either the Doxology, "Praise God, from Whom All Blessings Flow" (*The United Methodist Hymnal*, 94 or 95) or the Gloria Patri, "Glory Be to the Father" (*The United Methodist Hymnal*, 70 or 71). Either of these hymns of praise would be appropriate.
- Allow five to seven minutes for the groups to do research. Then reconvene as a large group and ask the groups to present their findings.
- With this perspective, work through the passages in Revelation where the glory of God is mentioned.
- Ask for class members' insights regarding God's wrath in this passage. (The unusual element is the association of the wrath of God with entering the Temple. The implicit purpose of the plagues is to bring the rebellious order to repentance [16:9 and 11], and thus into a liberated, cleansed, healed, and transformed life with God. It would seem, therefore, that John's image of no one being able to enter the Temple until the plagues were completed is meant to convey the fact that nothing unclean can enter into the presence of God.)
- Explain that John sees this reality in other images in the vision. In 21:27, John sees that "nothing unclean will enter it (New Jerusalem, where God's presence dwells), nor anyone who practices abomination or falsehood." And in 22:15, he sees that "outside are the dogs and sorcerers and fornicators and murderers and idolaters, and everyone who loves and practices falsehood."
- Also explain that John seeks to give us a radical image here. There is no compromise with the holiness of God.

We cannot retain anything in our lives contrary to our perfect wholeness and live in the presence of God.

- After discussing the above information allow a few moments for quiet reflection. Then ask these questions for reflection:
—When or where have you experienced the holiness of God, those quick glimmers of God?
—Can we prepare ourselves to enter into God's holy presence? How?
—What sins must you rid yourselves of before entering into God's presence?

(G) Where is God in all this?

- Share the following information with your class members then offer a time of reflection. If your class members feel comfortable talking about their spiritual lives encourage conversation in pairs.
  NOTE: if your class has a number of new people or has not had much conversation about their spiritual lives, this activity may be too risky to begin here.
     Another aspect of the bowls of wrath deals with the presence of God in our lives. Most people believe that God is present with them when they are "good." They may think that God is happy with them when their lives are more or less compatible with what they think God desires.
- Ask:
—When in your lives, during your "good" times, have you felt God's presence?
- Mention that the other side of this perspective is that God is angry with them and is removed from them in those areas where they are not "right" with God. Ask:
—Have you ever felt that you were out of favor with God? If so, when?
- Continue by stating that John's vision seems to give us a powerfully altered perspective. John seems to see that it is precisely at the points of our darkness, our brokenness, our bondage to destructive powers in our lives that God is most actively present and at work. This work may be extremely painful. It may trouble us, disturb us, turn our world upside down. But God desires to bring us to that point of repentance where transformation into wholeness can take place. Ask:
—Have you ever met God in your brokenness or during despair?
—If so, what was that meeting like?
- Close with the singing of a hymn. "Trust and Obey" (*The United Methodist Hymnal*, 467) would be appropiate.

(H) Speculate on the cup of the LORD.

- For this learning option bring to class a variety of cups and glasses. Set these on the table. Try to include some silver, some with ornate designs, and if possible a Communion

chalice. Show photographs or drawings of some ancient cups.(These illustration can be found in various Bible dictionaries and other biblical resources.) Also bring a Bible dictionary that has an entry on *cup*, giving some of the historical background on this common drinking utensil.

- Divide the class members into small groups. Assign these groups one or two of the following Scripture passages to read and report back their findings: Genesis 40:11; 44:2; Psalm 11:6; 23:5; 116:13; Matthew 20:22; 26:39; Luke 22:20; 1 Corinthians 11:25.
- Ask each group to report their findings. You may also want to give historical information found in the Bible dictionary.
- Read aloud Revelation 16:19.
- Speculate together how you think the church of John's day would have related to the use of the term *cup*. Ask:
—How do you think they would see *cup of the Lord*?
—As they drank of this cup and lived out its implications in their lives in the midst of Fallen Babylon, would they not become the presence of the holiness of God in the midst of Fallen Babylon?
—Would they not be a reminder of God's response to the rebellion?
—Would they not become a disorienting presence in the life of Fallen Babylon?

Additional Bible Helps

A City in Three Pieces
For John, there may have been a practical illustration in the vision of the city split into three parts. Following the suicide of Nero in A.D. 68, the Roman Empire erupted in civil war. Rome (the historical particularization of Fallen Babylon for John) was divided into three factions contending for the rule of the Empire, and the cities of the Empire were brought to a standstill awaiting the outcome of the struggle. A large portion of Rome was burned in the battles between the rival factions. John may well have seen this as a historical manifestation of the reality of the true state of Fallen Babylon.

   Later, in the kings of the earth (18:9-10), John may be seeing both the deep dimensions of the fallenness of Babylon and its historical particularization. When a large portion of Rome was burned during the civil wars, the rulers of vassal nations, the economic power brokers, and the commercial interests were profoundly disturbed at what appeared to be Rome's sudden downfall. The vision may have been employing this event as an illustration of just how fragile and insecure are the historical manifestations of Fallen Babylon. If mighty Rome, invincible, all-powerful, queen of the entire Mediterranean, could be brought overnight ("in one hour"—18:10) to such a state of chaos, what does this say about the deeper realities that Rome incarnated?

11

Revelation 17:1–19:10

$\mathcal{T}$HE AGONY OF DEFEAT

LEARNING MENU

Keep in mind the ways in which your class members learn best as you choose at least one learning activity from each of the three Dimensions.

Dimension 1: What Does the Bible Say?

(A) Work with the study book questions.

1. What should be considered is whether John's notes of being in the Spirit are another signal that what we are dealing with here is a single, tremendous, unitary visionary experience of such depth and magnitude that John has to "break it out" into digestible portions for the comprehension of his readers.

Additional Discussion: The brief article in Additional Bible Helps, "Life in the Spirit" offers additional information for discussion.

2. For John the "whore" was the Roman Empire. The obvious implication of the whore as the "mother of whores" is that there are to be ongoing generations of the whore. The Roman Empire is only one historical incarnation of the whore. There are many more to follow.

3. Talk about biting the hand that feeds you! It would appear that two dynamics are present in the fact that the beast is both the foundation of the whore and the source of her destruction.

—The whore is a finite, historical, human incarnation of the dragon's rebellion. As such, each such incarnation comes to an end. It is then replaced by the next incarnation of the whore. This is the significance of the whore being the mother of whores.

—Fallen Babylon carries within itself the seeds of its own destruction. It is the inner structure of the relationship of the whore with the beast that brings about her demise.

4. What is implied is "now but not yet." One of the standard features of systematic theology is the theory of the kingdom of God as both a present reality and future hope. In one sense, the Kingdom was inaugurated in the incarnation of Christ. In another sense, it will be fully consummated at the end of history. John seems to be seeing the same perspective applied to the dragon's kingdom. It is already a "fallen" order, but its fallenness will be fully consummated in the future.

(B) Take a closer look at the introduction and the conclusion.

- Divide your class members into two groups. Supply each group with a large sheet of paper or posterboard, markers, and tape.
—Ask **Group One** to study Revelation 17:1-3 and 21:9-10.
—Ask **Group Two** to study Revelation 19:9-10 and 22:6-9.
- Ask each group the following questions:
—What do you observe in these passages?
—What do you think John is signaling to his readers?
- After the groups have completed their individual assignments, come back together as one group and ask students to compare the two passages and share their findings. Write the discoveries on the paper. What should be noted is a high degree of parallelism between the introductions and the conclusions to the visions of the whore (17:1–19:10) and the bride (21:9–22:9). Some of the following observations should be made.

The introductions (17:1-3 and 21:9-10):
—In both places "one of the seven angels who had the seven bowls" initiates the action.
—In both cases John notes that the angel "came and said to me . . ."
—In both places the angel says "Come, I will show you . . . ."
—Both times John reports that "in the spirit he carried me away . . . ."
In the Greek text of these introductions are twenty-six words identical in grammatical form and syntactical use.

The conclusions (19:9-10 and 22:6-9):
—Both conclusions begin with John reporting that the angel, "said to me . . . ."
—In both cases the angel first says to John: "These are true words . . ." (19:9b); "These words are . . . true . . ." (22:6).
—John's response to the angel in both places: "I fell down to worship at the feet of the angel . . ." (22:8); "I fell down at his feet to worship him . . ." (19:10).
—John reports both times: "but he said to me, 'You must not do that! I am a fellow servant with you and your comrades . . . . Worship God!' "
Interestingly, here again in the Greek there are twenty-six words with exactly the same form and function in both places.

- In the closing comments on this learning option make sure the following ideas are mentioned in the discussion:
The conclusions of the visions of the whore (19:9b-10) and the bride (22:8-9) are remarkably similar. Why does John disobey in 21:9-10 a direct order received in 19:9-10? The answer is that he doesn't! The introductions (17:1-3; 21:9-10) and the conclusions of the two parts of the vision suggest

that John is seeing one tremendous vision that he has to break into three pieces to describe for his readers. It is at the conclusion of this single vision that John, as at the beginning of his vision (1:17), was overwhelmed and fell at the feet of the angel.

(C) Consider whether Fallen Babylon is drunk with power today.

- Remind the class that John sees that the whore "was drunk with the blood of the saints and the blood of the witnesses to Jesus" (17:6).
- For this learning option you will need large sheets of paper, newspapers and/or news magazines, markers or crayons, scissors, glue, and tape.
- Divide class members into small groups. Supply each group with newspapers and art supplies. Ask each group to look through the newspaper or news magazines for examples of injustice. Cut out these pictures or articles and glue to the paper in random fashion, creating a collage.
- Next assign each group several of the passages below to read. Say: "In these passages in Revelation John sees the rebellious order killing God's people in 2:13; 6:9-10; 11:7; 12:17; 13:7, 15; 16:6; 19:2; and the implication of death in 2:10."
- Discuss in your small groups what appears to be the unlimited power of Fallen Babylon over New Jerusalem.
- Allow time for this discussion. Then ask:
—Can you think of examples of the martyrdom of Christians in our own time at the hands of an historical incarnation of Fallen Babylon, or other cases where the state operated with impunity against the Christian community? Include these names, situations, or a symbol for the event on your group's collage.
- Ask the groups to tape their collages on the wall. Recruit a representative from each group to highlight its work.
- Conclude with the following information: What John seems to be seeing is that in human history Fallen Babylon seems to have all the power. More than that, Fallen Babylon often thinks it can simply eradicate individual Christians or the Christian community that stands as disturbing and disruptive reminders of Fallen Babylon's dehumanizing and destructive values and structures. In this sense Fallen Babylon is drunk with the blood of the saints.

(D) Now you see it, now you don't; now you do, now you don't.

- Supplies for this learning option should include paper, pencils, markers, or crayons.
- Read aloud 17:8a. "The beast that you saw *was* [now you see it], and *is not* [now you don't], and *is* about to ascend

from the bottomless pit [now you do] and *go* to destruction [now you don't]" may raise questions on the part of the class.

- Share the following explanation with the class: The only explanation that has integrity with the rest of the vision is to relate this to what happens to Satan in 20:1-10. Satan is also the dragon (12:9; 20:2) who has given his power, throne, and authority to the beast (13:2). Whatever happens to the representative of the dragon also happens to the dragon.

    By implication, before Satan was bound (20:2), he was "free," or, in the imagery of 17:8, he "was." It would seem obvious that once he is bound and cast into the pit, that he "is not," although deeper dimensions of this reality will be seen in the next session. The fact that the beast next ascends from the bottomless pit further implies that the condition of being "is not" associated with being in the pit. In 20:7, John sees Satan "released" from the pit. This "release" seems to be a clear parallel to the ascent from the pit in 17:8. The purpose of this "release" in 20:7, however, is that Satan and his hoards might be thrown into the lake of fire (20:10), which certainly equates with going to destruction in 17:8.

- Divide your class members into small groups. Ask them to draw or diagram this sequence of events as the following verses are read slowly: 17:8 and 20:7, 10.
- After allowing several minutes for your groups to work, invite them to show their diagram to the whole class. Ask:
—What message do you think John is trying to convey? (Here John seems to be seeing 17:8 as the overarching reality of the rebellious order and 17:11 represents its particularized incarnation in the history of Rome. Yet even in the face of the apparent invincibility of the whore, the vision reveals that her foundation is fatally flawed.)

(E) Explore the use of sexual imagery in Revelation and other biblical books.

Many sexual references and imagery appear in the Book of Revelation. These references are not only found in Revelation but in the many books of the Bible. At first we may feel very uncomfortable with this imagery and references, not quite knowing how to interpret their meanings. This learning option will look at various Scripture passages that use sexual imagery and research their history and meaning.

- For this learning option you will need a concordance, paper, pens or pencils, a Bible dictionary (include prostitution listings), commentaries including—Numbers, Judges, Jeremiah, Ezekiel, Hosea, Isaiah, Nahum, and Revelation.
- Divide your class members into four groups.
- Supply each group with appropiate research resources, paper, and pens. Group four will need paper, crayons, and pencils.
- Make the following group assignments.
Group One—Using a Bible dictionary, research historical information on prostitution.

—Was prostitution generally accepted by Old Testament Jewish tradition and law?
—What was cultic prostitution?
—What occurred under the reform mentioned in 2 Kings 23?
Group Two—Look up the following Scripture passages and read in the commentaries, if available: Numbers 25:1-2; Judges 2:13, 17; 8:27, 33; and Jeremiah 3:6.
Group Three—Look up the following Scripture passages and read in the commentaries, if available: Ezekiel 6:9, 16, 23; Hosea 4:12; Isaiah 23:16; and Nahum 3:4.
- Ask Groups Two and Three the following questions:
—What is going on in these passages?
—How is the term *harlot* used in your Scripture passages?
—Is the literary figure of speech called "personification" involved?
—If so, how?
Group Four—Look up the following Scripture passages and read in a commentary, if available: Revelation 17:1-6.
- Using the information in the study book (pages 99-100), illustrate the image given in your passage.
- Share with this group the information in the Additional Bible Helps article, "Fornication."

- Allow ten to twelve minutes for study and research; then ask the groups to report back to the whole class.
- Discuss the following questions with your class:
—Does reading this strong sexual language from the Bible surprise you?
—The words *harlot*, *prostitute*, or *whore* are often used to refer to a broken relationship with God (or often in the Old Testament a broken relationship with Israel). Does this fact surprise you?
- Offer the following information to the class:
    Unfortunately most of the negative sexual personifications used in the Bible are feminine. We must be sensitive when using these images, realizing that they are images and are inclusive. In other words the images in reference include the unfaithfulness of both the men and women. (If your class members would like to study in more detail the uses of feminine imagery in the Old Testament, look at the leader's guide of volume 7 of this Journey Through the Bible Series, pages 68-69.)

Dimension 3: What Does the Bible Mean to Us?

(F) Get out while the getting is good!

As we can see from the letters to the churches, one of the most difficult aspects of Christian discipleship is how to live as citizens of God's New Jerusalem in the midst of a Fallen Babylon world. Only two of the seven churches seem to be succeeding (Smyrna and Philadelphia). The church is always tempted to "baptize" the culture in which it is immersed rather than be an agent of transformation within that culture.

● For this learning option you will need a large sheet of paper, markers, and tape, or chalkboard and chalk.

● Have the class members develop a list of the major values and perspectives of the differing cultures (local, state, national, ethnic, and so forth) in which they live. For instance, "machismo" might be a powerful cultural value in a Hispanic community. Football or basketball might be a primary social force in the city in which the church exists. The "good ol' boy's" club may run the political or economic structure of the community. This is only a minute sampling of what the list could contain. More complex issues such as abortion, euthanasia, and homosexuality can also be added.

● Have the class members identify those items on the list that they believe are clearly contrary to life as a citizen of New Jerusalem. Ask:

—In light of those items, where does your congregation stand?

—Is your congregation simply incorporating those values into its life or does it stand as a liberating and transforming alternative to the destructive brokenness and dehumanizing bondages of its culture? If so, how?

● Say: "Unless the church heeds the call to 'come out of her, my people, so that you do not take part in her sins,' it will compromise its testimony to Jesus Christ. Like Laodicea, it will become 'lukewarm,' adopting the temperature of its culture, becoming a thermometer rather than a thermostat."

● Ask the class to discuss this aspect of the cost of Christian discipleship. Ask:

—When have you felt the tension between what culture "tells" you and what you understand Christian discipleship calls you to be or do?

—Has your congregation struggled with this tension? If so, how?

(G) The economy is the issue.

● Divide your class members into four groups. Supply each group with one of the following references from John's vision.

● In preparation for the session, make a list of the portions of John's vision that relate to economic matters. Write one reference per sheet of paper. This list can include the following:

—**Group 1:** The Laodicean church: "For you say, 'I am rich, I have prospered, and I need nothing' " (3:17).

—**Group 2:** The third horseman: "Its rider held a pair of scales in his hand, and I heard what seemed to be a voice in the midst of the four living creatures saying, 'A quart of wheat for a day's pay, and three quarts of barley for a day's pay, but do not damage the olive oil and the wine!' " (6:5-6).

—**Group 3:** The beast from the earth: "no one can buy or sell who does not have the mark, that is, the name of the beast or the number of its name" (13:17).

—**Group 4:** The merchants of the earth in 18:11-17 and 18:23 (and perhaps the shipmasters in 18:17-19).

● After the small groups have looked at the Revelation references, ask them to look at the economic reorientation that was manifested in the life of the early church (Acts 2:44-45; 4:32-37) as well as the first spiritual "break downs" in the Christian community in Jerusalem (Acts 5:1-10; 6:1).

● Ask each group to share their insights. Discuss why and how spirituality tends to manifest itself in the economic realm.

(H) Partake of a wedding feast.

● The purpose of this learning option is to help your class members feel the call of the church as the bride of Christ. This image is central (19:9) in John's vision.

● Prior to class time gather the makings of a simple, symbolic banquet: white tablecloth, glass serving containers, candles, glittery tinsel-type decorations, balloons, loaf bread, fruit, nuts, dried fruit, bubbly grape juice, colorful napkins, or goblet glasses (these come in plastic). Keep these banquet items hidden from your class members until you are ready to set the feast. Then make your simple meal feel like a celebration.

● Divide your class members into three groups. Ask each group to read its Scripture passages, look for marriage imagery, and be prepared to report back to the whole class.

—**Group One**—Hosea 2:16-20; Isaiah 54:4-8; Ezekiel 16:8

—**Group Two**—Mark 2:19; John 3:27-29

—**Group Three**—2 Corinthians 11:2

● Hear from the small groups on their findings. Be sure to incorporate information from the article, "Of Brides and Banquets," in the Additional Bible Helps when appropriate. Close with the marriage image found in Revelation 19:9a.

● Either lead the class members to another room where the banquet is set or ask them to help you prepare the feast to which they are all invited. Remind the class that as members of the church we are called to be the bride of Christ. This banquet is given for us.

● Either sing a hymn to begin the banquet or do so while preparing the banquet. A suggested hymn is "The Church's One Foundation" (*The United Methodist Hymnal*, 545).

● During the banquet reflect on what it means to be the "bride" of Christ. Ask: How do we live out this call?

Additional Bible Helps

Life in the Spirit

John indicated that his visionary experience began "in the spirit" (1:10); continued "in the spirit" (4:2); and now appears to conclude "in the spirit" (17:3). John seems to be indicating that the entire vision is one holistic, unified experience "in the spirit." He may also be recalling the essential nature of his experience at the three crucial points of the vision:

- *First*, his entry "in the spirit" into the visionary experience, which opens him to the presence of the risen Christ and Christ's message to the church (1:10–3:22);
- *Second*, his movement "in the spirit" into heaven where he sees the worship of God and the Lamb and the disclosure of the scroll of God's response to the rebellion (4:1–16:21);
- *Third*, his movement "in the spirit" to the desert (17:3) and mountain (21:10) where he sees the nature of the two orders of being that result from God's response to the rebellion.

Earth and Sea

It is interesting to speculate about the role of the earth and the sea in 18:9-19. The kings of the earth are not new; they represent the human leadership of the historical particularizations of Fallen Babylon. Their concern is with the *structures* of power that enable them to exercise leadership and control.

The merchants of the earth obviously are involved in the life of the rebellious order. Their concern is the *value system* of Fallen Babylon that enables them to prosper.

What about those whose livelihood links them to the sea? Does the sea here represent the rebellious realm as the earth appears to do with the kings and merchants? Does the sea represent the *functional dynamics* of Fallen Babylon that enliven and incarnate both its *structures* and its *value system*?

Of Brides and Banquets

The image of the church as bride is not original with the vision. Even in the old covenant the relationship between God and Israel is described as that of the bride and her husband (Hosea 2:19; Isaiah 54:5-6; Ezekiel 16:8). Jesus employed the image in his teaching to express the relationship between himself and his disciples (Mark 2:19) and to describe his return. Paul also uses the image when he tells the Corinthians he betrothed them to Christ as a pure bride to her one husband (2 Corinthians 11:2); when he reminds the Romans that their old husband, the law, is dead and that they now belong to another, Christ; and when he uses the relationship between Christ and the church as the epitome of the marriage relationship. The bride image, then, would most likely have been a familiar one to John's readers.

The blessing for those invited into the marriage supper of the Lamb (19:9a) is the central blessing of the seven blessings in the vision. Three have preceded and three are to follow. It is now possible to see more clearly the theme of the blessings. The wedding image includes the images of pure clothing and righteous deeds. Each of the blessings relates

directly to these two elements. The first and sixth blessings are for those who do the words of the prophecy, that is, for those whose "deeds" witness to their New Jerusalem citizenship. The second and fifth blessings have to do with death. In the fifth blessing, those of the first resurrection have "come to life" but not the "rest of the dead" (20:4 and following). In the second, however, there is also the mention of the "deeds" of those who die in the Lord. The third and seventh blessings are concerned with the "clothes" of the faithful, keeping them and washing them. Through the blessings, therefore, the vision emphasizes the crucial importance of the "garments/deeds" of the saints, and draws them together in the vision of the bride and the wedding banquet.

The Use of Numerical Images in Hebrew Culture

Like the numbers three and seven, in the Hebrew image pool ten was a number representing fullness, totality, completeness.

For instance, in Genesis 18:32, God would spare Sodom if ten righteous men could be found in it. The reason is due to the basis for the "minim" in the Jewish tradition—that is, there had to be at least ten Jewish males before there could be an official assembly of the community. In the rabbinic tradition we find that towns would often secure the services of ten elderly men who would always be on "standby" to provide the "minim" in case there was an urgent need to decide some community issue. Another example: the wilderness tabernacle was enclosed with ten curtains (Exodus 26:1). Of course, the premiere example is the Ten Commandments.

It is futile to attempt to interpret this image as ten literal, historical kings or nations (such as one earlier interpretation in this century saw the common market as the fulfillment of the image). Rather John seems to be seeing that there will be a "complete" history of the rebellious order, all of which will be under the power of the beast.

Fornication

Fornication is one of the chief attributes of Fallen Babylon. Later in the vision Fallen Babylon is the whore (17:1, 15, 16; 19:2), the mother of whores (17:5) with whom the kings of the earth have fornicated (17:2; 18:3, 9). The wine of her fornication has made drunk those who dwell upon the earth (17:2) and the nations (18:3) so that the earth was corrupted by her fornication (19:2).

Biblically speaking, *fornication* has a predominately religious dimension. Fornication was the rejection of God for the worship of other gods. The essence of Fallen Babylon, therefore, is that it seduces people into the rejection of God and into the worship of the beast. In both Pergamum and Thyatira, the accommodation of the church to Fallen Babylon is described as "fornication" (2:14, 20-21).

12

Revelation 19:11–21:8

THE LONGEST VICTORY

LEARNING MENU

Keep in mind the way in which your class members learn best as you choose at least one activity from each of the three Dimensions.

Dimension 1:
What Does the Bible Say?

(A) Work with the study book questions.

TEACHING TIP

Before the class, review for yourself the role of "robes" and "clothes" from the materials in session 3 of this leader's guide, page 14. You might also review the materials on the "white robe" from session 5, pages 25-26. If you kept notes from those class sessions, review them and bring them to class; reintroduce this information in the class discussion when appropriate.

1. The object of this question is to determine whose blood is on the robe of the rider. Since robes and clothing are used in the vision to describe the outward manifestation of a per-

son's nature, it would follow that the robe of the rider expresses something of the manifestation of his nature. It would seem that John is seeing here another image of the Crucifixion. Therefore, the blood is Jesus'.

2. It would be easy to miss John's note about the beast and false prophet being thrown alive into the lake of fire. At this point in the recounting of the vision, it is only necessary to note its presence and to keep the puzzle in mind. The solution comes to light in the next section of the vision where John sees the binding of Satan.

3. John's vision reveals that the "second death" is being cast into the lake of fire, and the "first resurrection" is coming to life in Christ as citizens of New Jerusalem. By speaking of a "second death" and a "first resurrection," however, the vision implies a "first death" and a "second resurrection." The implication of a "first death" does not have a simple answer. There are two options:

• it means the physical death that ends a person's historical existence, in which case the "second death" would be the final disposition of those who worship the beast and its image;

• it means the spiritual death that characterizes Fallen Babylon and out of which the redeemed are raised by the "first resurrection," in which case the "second death" is the consummation of that state of death.

The implication of a "second resurrection" may not be as mysterious as the "first death." John sees that those who do not partake of the "first resurrection" do not come to life until the end of the millennium (20:5). This suggests that the "second resurrection" is the raising of the citizens of Fallen Babylon for the Final Judgment.

Additional Discussion: John's vision of a first resurrection is not unusual. Have the class look at some of Paul's use of resurrection imagery for Christian experience (Romans 6:4; 8:11; Ephesians 2:6; Colossians 2:12; 3:1).

Dimension 2: What Does the Bible Mean?

(B) Discover the attributes of the rider on the white horse.

● Put the following list of attributes of the rider on the white horse (19:11-16) on a large sheet of paper before the class gathers. Print the attributes down the left side of the paper and the list of Scripture references (all from Revelation) down the right side of the paper (as they appear in this printed list). Then fold over the left side of the paper so that only the Scriptures and group headings are visible.

Group One:	
—Faithful	1:5; 2:10, 13; 3:14; 17:14; 21:5; 22:6
—True	3:7, 14; 6:10; 15:3; 16:7; 19:2, 9; 21:5; 22:6
—Righteous	22:11
Group Two:	
—Judge	6:10; 11:18; 16:5; 18:8; 18:20; 19:2; 20:12, 13
—Warrior	2:16; 12:7; 13:4; 17:14
—Eyes like a flame of fire	1:14; 2:18
Group Three:	
—Head with diadems	12:3; 13:1
—Robe dipped in blood	1:5-6; 5:9; 7:14; 12:11; 3:4, 5, 18; 4:4; 16:15
—The Word of God	1:2, 9; 6:9; 17:17; 20:4
Group Four:	
—Sharp sword from his mouth	1:16; 2:12, 16; 19:21
—Rule with a rod of iron	2:27; 12:5
—Tread the winepress	14:19-20
—King of Kings and Lord of Lords	1:5; 15:3; 17:14; 21:24

● Divide your class members into four groups. Assign the Scripture passages on the list. Ask each group to read the references and to discover the attributes given in each section.
● After allowing several minutes for the groups to work, ask them what they have found. Ask:
—Do your findings correspond with the list on the left-hand side of the chart? (Unfold the paper revealing the list of attributes.)

—How do these attibutes of the rider on the white horse broaden our grasp of John's vision of Jesus as the triumphant warrior?
—What are your feelings about thinking about Jesus as a "warrior"?
—Is "warrior" a new image of Christ for you?

(C) Compare Ezekiel's vision and John's vision of God's battle.

● For this learning option you will need paper, pens or pencils, and a commentary on Ezekiel. Also you will need a large sheet of paper and markers, or chalkboard and chalk.
● Briefly speak to the group on the topic of instant victory.
   In the recent history of the Middle East, six-day wars have shrunk to 100-hour wars. But neither seems to approach the instantaneous war of the rider against the beast and the kings of the earth. In an instant the scene moves from the mobilization of the forces of rebellion (19:19) to their utter defeat (19:20-21).
● Allow some time in class for your class members to read silently the following Scripture passages: Revelation 19:11-21 and Ezekiel chapters 38 and 39.
● Then ask the following question. (Write on a large sheet of paper or on the chalkboard.) If some of Ezekiel's images are unclear, refer to a commentary.
—What images and events in Ezekiel do you see in Revelation?
   Be sure to point out the following:
—Ezekiel's vision of Gog and Magog is much more detailed than John's.
—Two points of similarity are (1) the gathering of the hosts of the earth against God's faithful and (2) the invitation to the birds of the air to come and feast upon the corpses. (Ezekiel envisions a battle between the forces of evil and God's people, but John sees no battle, only the victory of the rider and the defeat of the beast and false prophet. John sees no battle possibly because for John's vision the victory has already been won by the Lamb slain from the foundation of the world.)
—Are there any shifts John made in his use of Ezekiel's imagery?

(D) What is the Millennium?

This portion of John's vision has been more divisive in the Christian community than probably any other passage of Scripture. Denominations have been split over the interpretation of the Millennium, and new sects have sprung up around its interpretation. It would be best to help the class look at what is actually in the text and let the text speak for itself without theological overlays.

To let the text speak for itself, however, will take some preparation because John used some grammatical indicators that usually get lost in translation into English. See the following box.

When studying the Millennium and its references in Revelation, the following information is most important. The first indicator is the absence of a definite article (*the*) with the first appearance of a thousand years. The Greek language is precise in its use of the definite article *the*. When a word appears without the article, the focus of attention is upon the character or quality of the thing being described. When a word has the article, the specific identity of the thing is the focus.

In the vision, the thousand-year period is first introduced as "thousand years" without the article (20:2), intimating that it is the character or quality of the period that is at stake. The next use has "*the* thousand years" (20:3), identifying this as the period introduced in the previous verse. When the time unit is introduced again in a new frame of reference in 20:4, it again appears as "thousand years" without the article, and is again followed by "*the* thousand years" (20:5), which identifies the second period as the one previously introduced. The last two appearances of the term in 20:6 and 7 identifies this as the period introduced back in 20:2 and 4. John is precise and consistent, therefore, in his use of articles in describing his vision of a thousand-year period.

John's usage, therefore, suggests that this period of time is also an image, a symbol, a pointer to something beyond itself.

• Explain the boxed information to your class members, being sure to give the text examples.
• Then ask three class members to read aloud the following Scripture passages where the term *one thousand years* appears:
—Psalm 90:4
—Ecclesiastes 6:6
—2 Peter 3:8 (New Testament reference quoting Psalm 90:4)
  These references are the only ones in the Bible outside of Revelation.
• Hence, biblically, the largest conceivable unit of time was a thousand years. These passages reflect the biblical perception of the extremes of temporal measurement, a day being the smallest and a thousand years being the largest units of time. The proof is found in Ecclesiastes 6:6, "Even though he should live a thousand years twice over . . . ." Instead of writing, "two thousand years," which would be expected as the simplest way to express such a unit of time, the writer uses the awkward phrase, "a thousand years twice." This confirms that the biblical perspective of time could not conceive of a period longer than a thousand years.
• With this additional biblical background reflect on how John must have been using this image relating to time. Ask class members for insights on this idea.

This information relating to John's pool of images for time indicates that John was seeing a huge portion of time, not a literal one-thousand calendar years.
• If John's thousand years are an image for a large period of time, then the events that initiate and consummate this period become extremely significant for our understanding of what this period represents.

(E) What begins the Millennium?

It is obvious that the Millennium begins with the binding of Satan (20:2). The question is, *What is the binding of Satan?* As noted in the study book, this image brings us back to the image of the beast and false prophet thrown *alive* into the lake of fire (19:20).
• Illustrate the images of the vision for the class by constructing a pyramid with four levels. At the top level put Fallen Babylon. The level below would contain the beast and false prophet. The third level down would have Satan, the dragon. The lowest level would represent Death and Hades:

• Explain the following:
  Death and Hades represents the entire realm of rebellion against God, the foundation of the whole structure of the rebellious order. Satan, of course, represents the "ruler" of that realm. As we have seen in session 8, the beast and false prophet represent the means by which Satan's rebellion is incarnate in human history. Fallen Babylon represents the human community held in the destructive and dehumanizing bondage of the rebellion.
• Illustrate this interdependent relationship by stacking four blocks on top of each other. (If possible have the blocks be different sizes, the largest block on the bottom.)
• Now have the class reflect on what would happen if the beast and false prophet were rendered powerless.
• Ask for ideas. (Satan's bondage over the citizens of Fallen Babylon would be broken and they would be liberated from that destructive imprisonment.
  (At this point pull out the second block from the top. The top block should no longer remain in the stack.)
• Then ask:
—Could this be what the vision is revealing in the beast and false prophet thrown into the lake of fire?

—But if they are still alive, as the vision indicates (19:20), is not there still the possibility they might exercise their destructive bondage over people?

● Read 20:1-3. Explain that what John is seeing is that while Satan's bondage over the citizens of Fallen Babylon has been broken by Christ, it is still possible for people to be held in that bondage *if they choose*—the beast and false prophet are still alive! John seems to be seeing why, if God has already won the victory in the death of the Lamb slain from the foundation of the world, the bondage of rebellion still holds people and nations in its dehumanizing grip.

● In review, bring out the following points:

—This also gives us more understanding of the "mortal wound that was healed" (13:3, 12, 14). The loss of the beast and false prophet is a mortal wound for the dragon (Satan), but they are still alive (healed) and able to imprison those who choose to enter into their rebellion against God.

—If the bloody robe of the victorious Christ who casts the beast and false prophet into the lake of fire is an image of the victory of the cross, then the cross is the "binding of Satan" and the inauguration of the Millennium.

Dimension 3: What Does the Bible Mean to Us?

(F) What ends the Millennium?

● The scriptural details of the Millennium (one thousand years) are very compacted. Therefore read slowly (or ask a class member to read) the following verses, pausing to ask a question, wait for the class members' response, then continue reading.

● Read Revelation 20:7.

—What brings the Millennium to an end? (The release of Satan from his prison brings the Millennium to an end.)

—Does Satan escape from his prison? (He is released, obviously by the one who put him there.)

—Who seems to be in control here, God or Satan? (God is in control of what is happening here.)

● Read 20:8.

—What might be the purpose for Satan's release? (Satan's release appears to be only for the purpose of consummating God's victory over the rebellious realm.)

● Read 20:9.

—Who surrounds "the camp of the saints and the beloved city"? (Satan and the followers.)

—Is there a long protracted battle? (No. It is another "instant victory," parallel to the one by Christ over the beast and false prophet.)

—What is meant by "camp of the saints"? And how does this differ from rapture theology? (In contrast to the popular and pervasive "rapture theology," the "camp of the

saints," God's faithful people, are at the center of the action right to the very end.)

—With God's faithful people being present at the end, what kind of relationship is suggested between God and God's people of faith?

(G) Who reigns with Christ through the Millennium?

● For this learning option bring a concordance, paper, and pens.

● Ask class members to use a concordance and to look at the presence of the words *throne* or *thrones* in John's vision. Ask:

—How many times is it used? (Of the forty-seven uses of the term in John's vision here is the breakdown: 40 refer to the throne of God and the Lamb; three refer to Satan's throne [2:13; 13:2; 16:10]; and of four remaining uses, three are the thrones of the twenty-four elders [4:4—twice, 11:16] and the other the thrones of those who reign with Christ in 20:4.)

● Relate the following information to the class.

The twenty-four elders represent the community of God's people (see the study book, chapter 4, page 35), those whom the Lamb has made a kingdom of priests (1:6, 5:9).

There were twenty-four courses of priests in the religious organization of the old covenant who served God continuously throughout the year.

Now, in his vision of the Millennium, John sees that those who reign with Christ are seated on thrones and are priests of God (20:6). Therefore, it seems that John is seeing a fuller depiction of what the twenty-four elders represent.

● After relating the above information to the class members, divide them into two groups:

Group One—Have this group study Ephesians 2:1-6, Paul's description of how citizens of Fallen Babylon (Ephesians 2:1-3) become citizens of New Jerusalem (Ephesians 2:4-6a) and their status: "seated us with him in the heavenly places in Christ Jesus" (Ephesians 2:6)!

● Ask the group to look closely at Revelation 20:4-6 and answer:

—Is John seeing in his vision the same thing Paul is describing?

Group Two—Have this other group study Luke 22:28-30, where Jesus indicates that judgment is to be given to his disciples. In the same context, ask them to look also at 1 Corinthians 6:2.

● Ask the two groups to come together and share their findings. Ask:

—What will be the status of the Christian disciples?

● Read aloud 20:4 from the New Revised Standard Version of the Bible. (Translations are not clear at this point because John's Greek is complex. You might want to compare with the author's translation:

"Then I saw thrones, and authority to judge was given to *those* seated on them, *both* the souls of those who had been beheaded for their testimony to Jesus and for the word of God, *and* those who had not worshiped the beast or its image and had not received its mark on their foreheads or their hands.")

This is a vision of martyrs in heaven and faithful disciples who are still in the midst of a Fallen Babylon world. It would seem that the latter group consists of Christian disciples in every age of history until the end.

(H) Sing Praises!

● In closing celebrate in the singing of several hymns. You will need enough hymnals for all your class members. (The number references are from *The United Methodist Hymnal*.) You will note that these hymns carry many of the images that we have been studying during our work in Revelation. If possible recruit a pianist ahead of time to accompany your class in singing these hymns.

● Tell the class to look for the now familiar images. Here are some suggestions for you to choose from:
"Lo, He Comes with Clouds Descending" (718)
"Let All Mortal Flesh Keep Silence" (626)
"Holy, Holy, Holy! Lord God Almighty" (64)
"This Is the Feast of Victory" (638)
"My Lord, What a Morning" (719)
"Fix Me, Jesus" (655)
"Crown Him with Many Crowns" (327)
"For the Healing of the Nations" (428)

Additional Bible Helps

The Word of Power

The phrase *Word of God* has been widely and deeply studied, both in its Jewish and Hellenistic settings. Among the numerous facets of meaning the phrase conveyed in both cultures was the idea of the ruling dynamics of the created order that related to the very nature of the deity. In the prevailing stoic worldview of the Roman Empire, the *Word* was the divine principle that ordered the inner structure of the universe. In the Jewish community the *Word* was the operative presence of God that brought the created order into being and that shaped human life and history. For both Jews and non-Jews, therefore, the phrase would have rich dimensions for their understanding of God's presence and activity in the world. The Gospel of John also identifies Jesus as the "Word," the very image and likeness of God that became flesh (John 1:1 and following). Perhaps the phrase has more significance for the faithful in the vision since they are

repeatedly described as those who have the "Word of God." This brings the church into the picture of the conquering Christ. If Christ is the "Word of God" and the church has the "Word of God," then the church is involved in the presence and work of Christ in the world.

Keeping Score

The idea of heavenly records was widespread. Moses asks to be blotted out of God's book if God will not forgive the people (Exodus 32:32). The psalmist asks God to blot the wicked out of the book of the living (Psalm 69:28). Paul speaks of his coworkers' names being written in the book of life (Philippians 4:3), and Jesus tells his disciples to rejoice that their names are written in heaven (Luke 10:20). In Daniel's vision of judgment, "books were opened" (Daniel 7:10), and God's people were those whose names are "written in the book" (Daniel 12:1).

The books other than the Lamb's book of life (Revelation 20:12) appear to be the records of works. First century Judaism had developed the idea of a "treasury of merits." This entailed a heavenly record of every good and evil deed a person did. Obedience to the law, faithful observance of the religious practices, covenant worship, pious deeds beyond the requirements of the law all built up one's credit balance.

On the debit side were all acts of disobedience, failure to observe the proper rituals, and all impious acts. The books would be tallied in the Judgment, and one hoped that the credit side would outweigh the debit side. This perspective is what lay behind the Pharisaic emphasis upon works of the law.

How do these two books relate to each other in the vision of the Judgment? Jesus gives an insight: "Not everyone who says to me, 'Lord, Lord,' will enter the kingdom of heaven, but only the one who does the will of my Father in heaven" (Matthew 7:21). Here Jesus seems to lean heavily upon works in obedience to the will of God rather than relationship with him as Lord. But he continues, "On that day many will say to me, 'Lord, Lord, did we not prophesy in your name, and cast out demons in your name, and do many deeds of power in your name?' " (Matthew 7:22) These people certainly seem to have the "works" that fulfill the will of God. It would appear that their records would insure them entry into the Kingdom. But Jesus replies, "I never knew you; go away from me, you evildoers" (Matthew 7:23). Although Jesus seems to start from a position of works over relationship, he ends by revealing that the works must be the consequence of relationship if they are to be valid. This is exactly what John sees in his vision. Unless one's name is written in the book of life, it appears that all the righteous deeds in the world will not suffice.

13

Revelation 21:9–22:21

*T*HE
THRILL OF VICTORY

Dimension 1:
What Does the Bible Say?

(A) Work with the study book questions.

1. Focus particularly on the following points in the comparison of heaven and New Jerusalem:
—the twenty-four-unit structure in both parts of the vision—the circle of twenty-four elders in chapter 4 and the square of twelve gates and twelve wall foundations in chapter 21;
—the presence of a four-part image—the four living creatures in chapter 4 and the foursquare city in chapter 21;
—the role of jasper in both places;
—the image of openness (4:1 and 21:25).

2. In preparation for this question, look also at Revelation 21:27, which provides the "connection" between the ever open gates (21:25) and those who are outside (22:15). Two issues, which should be discussed by the class, are raised by this image:

—the ever open gates suggest that entrance into God's New Jerusalem is always available to those outside;
—the restrictions upon who may enter seem to indicate that transformation is necessary for those outside to enter into the Holy City. People cannot bring their sin, those habits of life and attitudes of heart that separate them from God, into New Jerusalem (22:14).

Additional Discussion: Discuss whether your church models this picture of New Jerusalem. Ask:
—Are "outsiders" welcomed into the fellowship of the church?
—At the same time, are people called to discipleship?

3. Prior to class you might want to prepare either a handout or a chart that can be posted containing the elements of Ezekiel's vision and those of John's regarding the river of the water of life. Some aspects of the visions that might be discussed include the following:
—Why does Ezekiel's river flow from the threshold of the Temple (Ezekiel 47:1) and John's from the throne of God and the Lamb (22:1)? (There is no Temple in New Jerusalem, God and the Lamb *are* its Temple [21:22].)
—Why does John's vision omit the river getting larger and deeper the farther it flows (Ezekiel 47:3-5)? In fact, why does John's river seem to be limited to New Jerusalem and not flow outside the gates? (There is no life outside New Jerusalem in John's vision, but all can come into the Holy City and drink the water of life [22:17] if they will leave their rebellion behind [22:14].)

—Why do Ezekiel's many trees on both sides of the river bearing fruit each month (47:7, 12) become for John a single tree of life that seems to straddle the river bearing twelve different kinds of fruit each month (22:2)?

NOTE: It might help to look at the "tree of life" image in Genesis 2:9 and, especially, 3:24. Could John be seeing that what was lost in the fall is now restored in New Jerusalem? See also the promise to the conquerors in Revelation 2:7, together with the role of the tree of life in 22:14 and 19.

—John's vision (22:1) simplifies Ezekiel's rather elaborate vision of the life-giving properties of the river (Ezekiel 47:8-10), but in both cases it is a river of the water of life.

—Why are Ezekiel's leaves simply for healing (47:12) while John's are for the healing of the nations (22:2)? (Ezekiel seems to be seeing the restoration of Israel as God's covenant people [note the distribution of the land to the twelve tribes that follows in Ezekiel's vision] but John is seeing God's redemption extended to all humanity.)

Dimension 2: What Does the Bible Mean?

(B) Imagine a rather large city.

The purpose of the exercise is to visualize for the class the fact that the New Jerusalem John sees coming down from heaven encompasses every known Christian community in existence at the time of John's vision. The point of the vision is that John's readers were participants in that New Jerusalem.

● You will need paper or clear plastic sheets (the type used for transparencies or report covers), pencils, and scissors.

● The map in the back of this leader's guide provides information about the locations of Patmos and the Roman Empire of the first century. Also compare the map in the study book (inside back cover) to find the locations of the early Christian communities. (The study book map can serve as an enlarged insert for the larger map found in this leader's guide.) Reproduce copies of this map for the class to do this exercise. Using the scale of the map, cut out from a piece of paper or plastic a square equivalent to 1,500 miles on each side of a point. Overlay this sheet on the map so that the island of Patmos is at the center of the open square.

● Ask the class to note the area covered. It contains all known Christian communities in the first century and most of the Roman Empire. Ask:

—What is John's vision revealing about New Jerusalem?

● Discuss what John might have seen if he were receiving his vision today. (Probably a city 8,000 miles on a side, or a cubic city that would enclose the entire globe!)

(C) Is it punishment or redemption?

● For this learning option you will need a large sheet of paper and marker or chalkboard and chalk. Also be sure to

read prior to class the article on page 69, "The Angel of the Bowls." Be prepared to share this information during the class discussion when appropiate.

● Divide your class members into two groups and make the following assignment:

Group One: Review the role of the angel in 17:1-3.

Group Two: Review the role of the angel in 21:9-10.

● Discuss as a class the question:

—What is the connection between these images?

● Some considerations for your preparation for such a discussion follow:

—We saw in session 10 that the plagues, the wrath of God, might be perceived as the love of God that burns against all that is destructive to God's beloved creation. It was also seen that the purpose of the plagues was not punishment but repentance.

—Also we saw in session 10 that the citizens of the rebellious order are characterized by their refusal to repent and thereby become citizens of New Jerusalem. This fact reinforces the fallen realm's refusal to repent, even when they see the consequences of their rebellion (session 6).

—It would seem, therefore, that both Fallen Babylon (the whore) and New Jerusalem (the bride) are formed by their response to the holiness of God. Fallen Babylon rejects God's overtures of redemption and experiences the destruction that comes from breaking itself against the ultimate reality of God. New Jerusalem, however, is peopled by those who repent of their rebellion and enter into the cleansing and healing presence of New Jerusalem. This makes it appropriate that one of the angels with the bowls of wrath should introduce the two cities formed by their response to the bowls.

● At this point add any information from the article, "The Angel of the Bowls," that was not brought out in the class discussion.

(D) Study differences between the Holy City and the Temple.

● For this learning option you will need various art supplies: markers, crayons, various colors of construction paper, tape, scissors, glue, glitter, ruler, and large sheets of paper or posterboard.

● Divide your class members into two groups.

Group One will work with Ezekiel's vision (Ezekiel 40–42).

Group Two will work with John's vision (Revelation 21–22).

● Be sure that each group has access to the art supplies. Instruct them to create a visual portrayal of their vision.

● Give the groups 10-15 minutes to work. Then ask a representative to show and explain their work.

● Be sure to note these two major differences between the visions of Ezekiel and John:

—Ezekiel's Temple has only three gates (East, North,

South), and one of those is permanently closed (East). This is an image of very limited access to the presence of God who dwells in the Temple. John, however, has three gates on each of the four walls of the city that remain always open. This is an image of unhindered access to the presence of God.

—While both Ezekiel and John's images are square, Ezekiel's Temple at about 750 feet on a side becomes minuscule in comparison to John's city, which is 1,500 miles on a side. Ezekiel's vision could almost be seen as an "enclave" against the nations who have taken Israel captive, while John's vision suggests God's city taking over the world.

● Be sure to display these creations on the classroom wall.

Dimension 3: What Does the Bible Mean to Us?

(E) Study images of the Holy City.

● For this learning option you will need large sheets of paper and markers or chalkboard and chalk, copies of *The United Methodist Hymnal*, paper, and pencils or pens. Also try to recruit a pianist or other instrumentalist to accompany your class members in singing this hymn at the conclusion.

● Begin with a general discussion of prophecy. Write these understandings on the chalkboard.

● After ideas have been recorded, share the following ideas:
   Prophecy is more than some kind of disclosure of the future. In fact, as has been seen, the prophecy of the vision has little to do with the future. Prophecy is the discernment and proclamation of the presence and purpose of God at work in the world. To keep the words of a prophecy, therefore, is to become involved in the disclosure of the presence and purpose of God. Christ's blessing, then, is for those whose lives in the world show the reality of God's presence and purpose in the midst of Fallen Babylon. The blessing is for those who live out their New Jerusalem citizenship and thus portray in their lives the reality of the vision. Ask:

—Is this definition broader than your own understanding?

—How do you feel about prophecy being the discernment and proclamation of the presence and purpose of God at work in the world?

● Divide the class into five groups and distribute copies of *The United Methodist Hymnal*. Ask the class members to turn to "O Holy City, Seen of John," 726. Ask each group to take a verse of the hymn, discuss the verse, and look for phrases, images, and so forth that they have studied.

● After allowing several minutes for small group discussion, ask each group to report back.

● Sing together this hymn.

(F) Research the history of Mount Zion.

● Prior to class sketch with a pencil a large, magnificent-looking mountain. You may even want to glue and sprinkle gold glitter on this mountain, this mountain of the Lord.

● Also prior to class time read the article in Additional Bible Helps, "A Mountaintop Experience."

● Gather the following supplies for the activity: felt-tip markers in a variety of colors and copies of *The United Methodist Hymnal* for class members to share.

● Tell the class that this learning option will be looking at the variety of titles, terms, and explanations concerning Mount Zion.

● Give class members one or two of the following Scripture references to look up. After finding the reference, instruct your class members to add to the picture by writing at the top of your pencil sketch the phrase from the Bible that describes Mount Zion. Suggested Scripture passages:

Joel 2:1; 3:17	Isaiah 52:1
Psalms 2:6; 48:1-2	Psalms 79:1
Isaiah 60:14	Isaiah 46:13
Psalms 43:3; 74:2	Isaiah 59:20; 60:14
Isaiah 8:18	Micah 4:1
Hebrews 12:22	Ezekiel 40:2
Galatians 4:26	Revelation 21:10

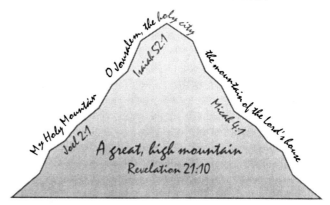

● Look at this mountain, discuss how together all these descriptions tell of its glory. At this time add any information from the article, "A Mountaintop Experience."

● Sing together "Marching to Zion" (*The United Methodist Hymnal*, 133.)

(G) Come!

● For the closing you will need copies of *The United Methodist Hymnal*.

● Share the following words of introduction:
   So many interpretations of Revelation build upon confirming the "righteous" in their favored status with God and condemning the "world" for its wickedness. There aren't many interpretations of Revelation that would make it a handbook for evangelization. Yet John's magnificent vision closes with an evangelistic appeal (22:17):

"The Spirit and the bride say, 'Come.'
And let everyone who hears say, 'Come.'
And let everyone who is thirsty come.
Let anyone who wishes take the water of life as a gift."

• Remind the class that one of the consistent elements in the letters to the seven churches was "Let anyone who has an ear listen to what the Spirit is saying to the churches." While the letters called the churches to faithfulness as citizens of New Jerusalem in their Fallen Babylon world, at the close of the vision the Spirit initiates the invitation to the world to come. The bride, of which the churches are a part, echoes the Spirit's invitation.

• Discuss the following question with your class members:

—How are the church and individual disciples called to radical New Jerusalem living in our Fallen Babylon world, yet, at the same time, called to bring the good news of redemption to that world?

• Bring out these points concerning the tensions that this dual responsibility bring:

—On the one extreme there is the response of the Ephesian-type church. It keeps itself completely unstained by its Fallen Babylon world, not allowing anything of Fallen Babylon to enter its community. But neither does it carry the transforming love of God into that world.

—On the other extreme there is the response of the Laodicean-type church. It is so involved with its Fallen Babylon world that it forgets its call to be the people of God and becomes a people of its culture. Is our church in between these two extremes like the types of churches found in Pergamum, Thyatira, and Sardis? (Remember that these churches try to maintain an unholy and unhealthy "balance" between the demands of radical discipleship and a compromise with the values and structures of its world.)

• Say: "It would seem that John's vision calls those who name Christ as Lord to live their lives in the world as such transformed citizens of New Jerusalem that those held in the destructive bondage of Fallen Babylon can see God's liberation incarnate in them and will themselves respond to the call to come to the water of life." Then ask:

—How well do you think our church is doing in responding to the call of God through John's vision?

—How well are you doing responding to God's call and living within the world?

—What are some of the more difficult trappings of culture to resist?

• Close by reading responsively the "Canticle of Hope," 734 in *The United Methodist Hymnal.*

Additional Bible Helps

The Angel of the Bowls
The bride of the Lamb, New Jerusalem, is revealed to John by the same angel that showed him the harlot of the beast, Fallen Babylon. Something of the synchronous nature of John's vision as well as its portrayal of an ongoing reality is seen in the description of the angel. Both here and in the introduction to the vision of the harlot (17:1-3), the angel is described as one of those "having " the seven bowls. Not "had" but "having," suggesting that the seven bowls are an ongoing reality that is intimately associated with the two women/cities.

In the vision of the seventh bowl God says, "It is done!" (16:17), exactly the same term God uses at the close of the vision of judgment (21:6). It seems that the seven bowls portray something of the fulfillment of God's purposes, which flows back into history from its consummation. As has been seen, the working of God's purposes in history has two radically different effects for Fallen Babylon and New Jerusalem. For one, God's presence is a torment, a disruption, a shaking of the foundations, a dissolution of its whole frame of reference, a death. For the other, God's presence is a joy, a healing, a transformation, a wholeness, a triumph, a life.

The vision of the bowls has also intimated that there is a redemptive purpose in God's presence, even though the rebellious order continues to blaspheme. While God's presence and action impact Fallen Babylon destructively, there is the possibility for its citizens to become citizens of New Jerusalem.

Thus the angel of the bowls is not merely a "stage prop" in the vision, but a vital and integral part of what John is seeing. The judgment of God shapes the life of both orders of being. This reality is imaged in the angel of the bowls who shows John the women/cities, which represent those two orders of being.

A Mountaintop Experience
Mount Zion, biblically, was God's holy mountain (Joel 2:1; 3:17; Psalms 2:6; 48:1-2); the site of the Temple, God's dwelling place (Isaiah 60:14; Psalms 43:3; 74:2; Isaiah 8:18). Mount Zion was also used as a synonym for Jerusalem, God's Holy City (Isaiah 52:1); and for the community of God's people (Psalm 79:1; Isaiah 46:13).

The biblical image of Zion as the mountain of God, the place of the Holy City of God and the community of God's redeemed people took on special significance when, in the light of the rebellion of God's covenant people, the prophets began to envision God's future restoration of the covenant community. In Isaiah's vision of the future community of God's redeemed people, God will come to Zion as Redeemer (Isaiah 59:20), and they will be called "the City of the Lord, the Zion of the Holy One of Israel" (Isaiah 60:14). In Micah's vision of the latter days, "The mountain of the LORD's house shall be established as the highest of the mountains" (Micah 4:1). In Ezekiel's vision he is taken to a very high mountain from which he views the future Temple/city (Ezekiel 40:2).

It appears that the early Christian community understood their experience with God in something of these terms. The writer of Hebrews affirms, "You have come to Mount Zion and to the city of the living God, the heavenly Jerusalem" (Hebrews 12:22). Paul reminds the Galatians, "the Jerusalem above; she is free, and she is our mother" (Galatians 4:26), and tells the Philippians that their commonwealth is in heaven (Philippians 3:20).

The vision of the Lamb on Mount Zion with the 144,000 faithful seems to resonate with the fulfillment of old covenant expectations, especially in light of the Temple/priestly imagery associated with the faithful. It also appears to be a preview of the greater vision of New Jerusalem that John now sees.

The "high mountain" to which John is taken in 21:10, therefore, may represent both Sinai, the mountain in the desert where God met and shaped a people into a covenant community; and Zion, the mountain where God's presence dwells with the covenant community in the Holy City.

Apostolic Foundation

The image of apostles as the foundations appears in Paul's perception of the citizenship of New Jerusalem:

"So then you Gentiles are no longer strangers and sojourners (alienated from the commonwealth of Israel), but you are joint citizens with the saints and members of the household of God, built upon the foundation of the apostles and prophets, Christ Jesus being the cornerstone, in whom the whole structure is joined together and grows into a holy temple in the Lord; in whom you also are built into it for a dwelling place of God in the Spirit." (Ephesians 2:11-12, 19-22).

Paul's use of apostles and Israel seems to carry the same perception as John's vision, even to the understanding of the new community as the dwelling place of God. The foundation of God's city/Temple is the apostles, but the entry is associated with Israel.

Jumbled Jewelry

The relationship of the jewels to the foundations of the walls is a puzzle. The foundations have already been identified as the apostles, and now they are each adorned with one of the jewels that appear on the breastplate of the high priest. The order of the jewels, however, has no correlation with the order of the twelve jewels on the breastplate.

Since the walls of New Jerusalem are the separation of holiness from unholiness, they are rightfully imaged as associated with the breastplate of judgment. The breastplate of the high priest was square and golden (Exodus 28:16). The high priest wore the breastplate when entering into the Holy of Holies to represent the twelve tribes before Yahweh (Exodus 28:29).

Where the image of the breastplate seems to break down is in its correlation with the twelve tribes of Israel (Exodus 28:21). In the first place, the twelve jewels are associated with the foundations (apostles), rather than with the gates (twelve tribes). Secondly, the order of the twelve jewels has no apparent correlation with the order of the breastplate or the tribes they represent, all, that is, except one. The fourth jewel, the emerald, is the only one in John's vision that

keeps its position in the breastplate (Exodus 28:18). The fourth tribe of Israel was Judah, the tribe of David, and the tribe of the root of David, the Lamb that was slain (Revelation 5:5). It seems that the vision is consistently placing its focus upon the tribe of Judah, the source of the Lamb.

How does this information aid the understanding of the jewels of the foundations as apostles? First, the apostles, throughout early Christian literature, are the apostles of the Lamb. In the synoptic accounts of Jesus' teaching, the twelve apostles are related to the twelve tribes: "Truly, I tell you, at the renewal of all things, when the Son of Man is seated on the throne of his glory, you who have followed me will also sit on twelve thrones, judging the twelve tribes of Israel" (Matthew 19:28; compare Luke 22:30). Thus the shift from the twelve tribes to the twelve apostles has its antecedent in the teaching of Jesus. The new covenant community is redolent with old covenant imagery, but it has a new foundation.

The Angelic Christ

When one remembers that the Lamb was the only one who is able to open the scroll of God's purpose (Revelation 5:5), it is not surprising that Christ is the angel who discloses to John the various aspects of the vision of God's purposes (22:6-7, 12-13, 16). But the angel who shows to John the whore and bride is described as one of the angels having the seven bowls (17:1; 21:9), who have been identified as the angels of the seven churches. How can this be? The most likely explanation is that the vision is picturing the nature of the relationship between the church and Christ.

In the first of the vision, John saw Christ in the midst of the seven lampstands (churches) and holding seven stars (angels of the churches). There is a close relationship between the church and Christ that is also imaged in the church having the "witness of Jesus." The vision suggests that the church incarnates Christ in the world. If this is the case, then it is possible to understand the angels with the bowls to be both the church and Christ.

Christ is intimately joined with the church in the continuation of God's response to Fallen Babylon. To worship Christ as though separate from the church would undermine the very essence of the church and perhaps raise the problem of placing Christ in competition with God as the focus of worship.

The Open Book

Apocalyptic books were usually "sealed" for disclosure at that later period of history when the message of the book would come to pass. For instance, Daniel is told, "The words are to remain secret and sealed until the time of the end" (Daniel 12:9). John is instructed not to seal up the prophecy (22:10), which indicates that it does not apply to a later period of history but to the present. This is made clear in the reappearance of the phrase found in the introduction, "the time is near" (1:3; 22:10).

$\mathcal{T}$HE STRUCTURE OF REVELATION

BY M. ROBERT MULHOLLAND, JR.

There is little agreement among scholars on the structure of Revelation. This seems strange in a book with so many clearly defined literary structures. The four series of sevens (the letters to the seven churches [2–3]; the seven seals [6:1–8:5]; the seven trumpets [8:6–11:18]; and the seven bowls [15:6–16:21]) stand out as the most clearly defined units. The section, 17:1–22:9, forms another clearly defined literary unit. The vision of God and the Lamb in heaven (4–5) forms another unit, defined by the two series of sevens that precede and follow. The central vision, 11:19–15:5, is defined by the seven trumpets and seven seals that bracket it and by the introductory/concluding bridges of the units (11:19–15:5) that are clearly linked through the imagery of the open Temple, which appears only here in Revelation.

It may well be that all attempts to set forth the structure of Revelation both fail and succeed at the same time. If the book is the literary portrayal of a vision, the written account of an altered state of consciousness, then it is a dynamic, extrinsic reality and not a static, intrinsic structure. The book is not simply a cognitive structure for conveying concepts, but also an affective dynamism for portraying an experience of reality.

The structure of Revelation is much like Ezekiel's vision of God: a wheel in a wheel (Ezekiel 1:16). Each object in the act has its own internal elements, which in turn are often related to the major or minor elements and actions of other parts of the vision.

Essential Dynamics of Relationship Among the Units of Revelation

The twelve units of Revelation can be viewed in the following way:

Introduction
(1:1-8)

Vision of Christ
(1:9-20)

The Seven Churches (2:1–3:22)	God and the Lamb (4:1–5:14)	The Seven Seals (6:1–8:5)
The Seven Trumpets (8:6–11:18)	The Big Picture (11:19–15:5)	The Seven Bowls (15:6–16:21)
The Harlot/Fallen Babylon (17:1–19:10)	Judgment in Christ (19:11–21:8)	The Bride/New Jerusalem (21:9–22:9)

The Conclusion
(22:10-21)

It might be assumed that this visual portrayal of the structure of Revelation is simply another static structural chart differing only in form from the more usual structural outline. Closer analysis reveals something of the dynamics of the vision. A central core of vision emerges from this structure. The inaugural vision of Jesus (1:9-20) is followed by a triad of heavenly visions in 4:1–5:14; 11:19–15:5; and 19:11–21:8, each of which contains the only notations of heaven being opened. John's initial vision of Jesus deepens and broadens out into the three-faceted heavenly vision that reveals the fullness of who Jesus is and what God has done in Christ. This book is "The Revelation of Jesus Christ" (1:1a).

Between the introductory vision (1:9-20) and the conclusion (22:10-21), the three groups of threes in Hebrew numerology form the perfection of perfection, or the ultimate wholeness of what is being portrayed. The last of the groups of threes gives the clue to the dynamic of relationship between the central core of heavenly vision and the other units of the vision. The harlot/Fallen Babylon (17:1–19:10) and the bride/New Jerusalem (21:9–22:9) form the first and third elements of a three-part unity that has the judgment of God in Christ as its central element. John's act of falling to worship the angel at the close of the synchronous vision gives the clue to the unity of these three parts as one great vision. The four groups of sevens relate to the core heavenly vision in a similar manner.

There is a high degree of relationship between the seven trumpets and the seven bowls. Both portray the ongoing consequences of the encounter between the realm of rebellion and the sovereignty of God. The context for this encounter is the story of Satan's rebellion and its consequences, which are depicted in the central heavenly vision (11:19–15:5). Thus, as the harlot/bride form the structural boundaries of the judgment of God in Christ, so also the seven trumpets and the seven bowls form the structural boundaries of the Big Picture.

The relationship between the seven churches and the seven seals is not so readily apparent as the relationship between the harlot/bride and the trumpets/bowls. Yet there is an inherent tie between them: both elements have as their primary focus the community of God's people (New Jerusalem) in the midst of the citizenship of the rebellious order (Fallen Babylon). The seven churches display the variety of responses of God's people to the fallen order, from almost total capitulation (Sardis and Laodicea) to apparently perfect discipleship (Smyrna and Philadelphia).

The numbering of God's people and their treatment at the hands of the rebellious order forms the major content of the seven seals (6:9-11; 7:1-17). Since God's people are focal in both series of sevens, it is no surprise that the core heavenly vision to which they are related portrays the worship of God and the Lamb in heaven. The community worshiping God in heaven is paralleled by the worshiping community of God's people in history. Thus, as with the other groups of threes, the seven churches and seven seals form the structural boundaries of the vision of God and the Lamb. Each three-part vision, therefore, has its own inherent dynamics that bond its heavenly core vision to the two other units that complete it.

There are also interconnecting dynamics between and among the nine elements that make up the three groups of three. For instance, the seven churches have a clear relationship with New Jerusalem, being the historical particularization of the citizenship of New Jerusalem in the midst of Fallen Babylon. The promises made to "those who conquer" find their fulfillment in the vision of New Jerusalem. The seven seals have several connections with other units: the numbering of the people of God in the interlude (7:1-17) is related to the worshipers of God in the interlude between the sixth and seventh trumpets (11:1); the last three horsemen (war, famine, death), together with the terror of the inhabitants of the rebellious order (6:12-17), have parallel elements in the account of the harlot (17:1–19:10); the first horseman is remarkably similar to the horseman of the judgment (19:11 and following); and the pouring out of a golden vessel upon the earth in the seventh seal (8:5) seems to have its larger counterpart in the pouring out of the golden bowls in 15:6–16:21, John's indication of being in the Spirit in the inaugural vision (1:9-20) is repeated in the first of the heavenly visions (4:2) and the introductions to the two parallel thirds of the final heavenly vision (17:3–21:10), perhaps an indication that the entire book is the representation of a single vision.

This is only a sampling of the varied interconnections that exist between and among the various units of John's vision. The full range of these internal dynamics of the vision will be explored in this study of Revelation. These examples suffice to indicate that Revelation portrays not simply a static, intrinsic, logical presentation of cognitive content but a dynamic, extrinsic, affective portrayal of an experience of the breadth, length, height, and depth of life in Christ.

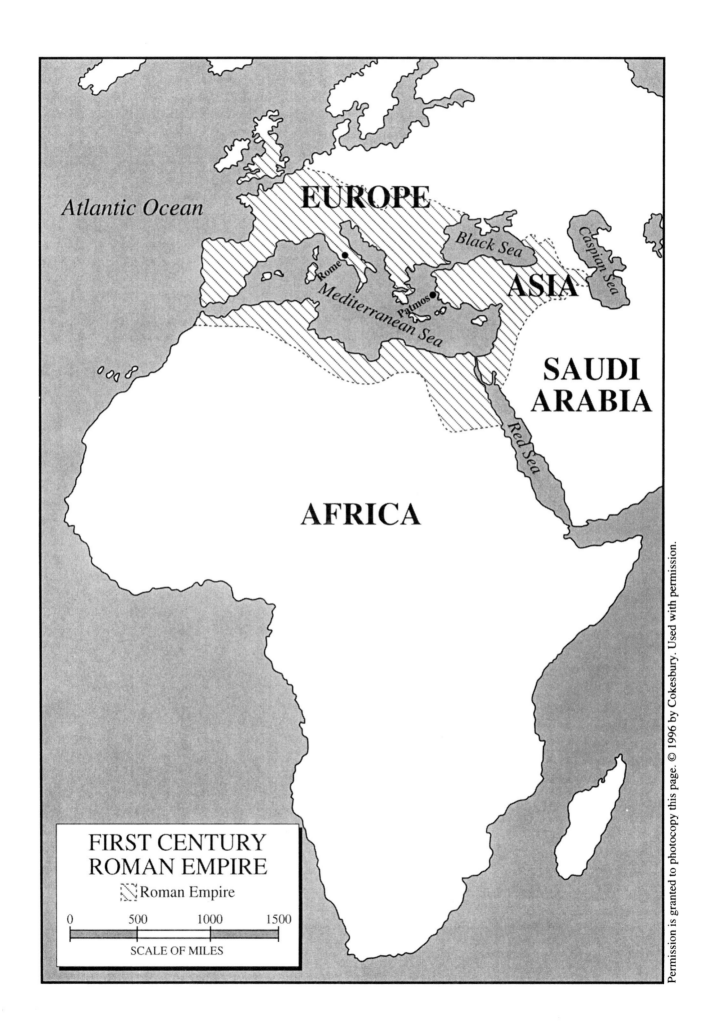

Atlantic Ocean

EUROPE

Black Sea

Caspian Sea

Rome•

ASIA

Mediterranean Sea

Patmos•

SAUDI
ARABIA

Red Sea

AFRICA

FIRST CENTURY
ROMAN EMPIRE

Roman Empire

| 0 | 500 | 1000 | 1500 |

SCALE OF MILES

CPSIA information can be obtained at www.ICGtesting.com
Printed in the USA
BVOW051131310512

291421BV00001B/27/P